REVELATION UNFOLDING

Also by Zack Mason

Killing Halfbreed
Shift
Chase
Turn
The Gospel According to Nature
Revelation Unfolding

REVELATION UNFOLDING

ZACK MASON

Dogwood Publishing
Lawrenceville, GA

Revelation Unfolding: Has the Antichrist Been Revealed?
Copyright © 2020 by Zack Mason

All Scripture quotations, unless otherwise indicated, are from the New King James Version of the Bible. Copyright © 1979, 1980, 1982 by Thomas Nelson, Inc. Used by permission. All rights reserved.

Scripture quotations marked (Amplified) are taken from the Amplified® Bible, Copyright © 1954, 1958, 1962, 1964, 1965, 1987 by The Lockman Foundation. Used by permission.

Scripture quotations marked (Young's Literal Translation) are taken from The Young's Literal Translation Bible (Public Domain).

Scripture quotations marked (ESV) are from The Holy Bible, English Standard Version® (ESV®), copyright © 2001 by Crossway, a publishing ministry of Good News Publishers. Used by permission. All rights reserved.

Scripture quotations marked (NIV) are taken from the Holy Bible, New International Version®, NIV®. Copyright © 1973, 1978, 1984, 2011 by Biblica, Inc.™ Used by permission of Zondervan. All rights reserved worldwide. www.zondervan.com The "NIV" and "New International Version" are trademarks registered in the United States Patent and Trademark Office by Biblica, Inc.™

Published in the United States by Dogwood Publishing, a division of More Than Books, Inc., Georgia. All rights reserved. No part of this publication may be reproduced, stored in a database or retrieval system, or transmitted in any form or by any means, except for brief quotations in printed reviews, without the prior written permission of the publisher.

ISBN-13: 978-0-9886524-4-6

Printed in the United States of America.
9 8 7 6 5 4 3 2 1
First Edition: August 2020

Cover Design by Matt Smartt

This book is dedicated to my King

THE LAMB OF GOD

WHO ALONE IS WORTHY

REVELATION UNFOLDING

The Prophecy Begins

THE DATE was July 15th, 2016.

Explosive news rocked the world that a military coup had broken out in Turkey.

Why was this such a big deal? After all, Turkey doesn't seem that important on the world scene. Why should it matter? And why should it matter *to you*?

As the bridge between Europe and Asia, Turkey wields enormous influence over European politics and NATO due to its strategic location and as a counterbalance to Russia and Iran. It controls the flow of trade goods, money, oil, and especially migrants from the Middle East to Europe, which makes it a nation of absolute strategic importance.

It also boasts the most powerful military in the Middle East and is consistently ranked in the top ten militaries globally. That, plus its key role in NATO, and the fact that it is home to a U.S. Air Force base (Incirlik) with over 50 nuclear weapons on site, makes the country of extreme national interest to the United States.

Spiritually speaking, it was the launching pad of Early Christianity, and today it holds the prophetic minds of Muslims across the world with a passionate grip. Historically, it also happens to be where the Roman Empire kept its capital for 1,000 years as well as being the land of the Ottoman, Assyrian, and Hittite Empires, all of which are biblically relevant.

Thus, many prophecies of the Bible reference it.

So, what about this coup? Why did it happen? What was it about and how does it relate to prophecy?

Even though Turkey is a Muslim nation, its modern secular military had always viewed itself as a protector of democracy and the civil rights of its people.

This time, significant elements of the Turkish army, navy, and air force believed that they needed to act to stop their president, Recep Erdoğan, from becoming a full-blown dictator before it was too late to stop his oppressive abuses of human rights.

But Erdoğan was ready for them.

In less than 24 hours, a strongly choreographed action between mosques, Muslim militia elements, and the rest of the Turkish government resulted in a complete shutdown of the coup before it got any traction.

Within days of the failed attempt, Erdoğan arrested or suspended 15,000 soldiers and police, 85 generals and admirals, 21,000 teachers, 1,500 university deans and rectors, 9,400 government workers (including 30 governors and 257 members of the Prime Minister's staff), 500 clerics and preachers, and many prominent journalists and judges.[1] He also forcibly closed over 2,000 Christian-run private hospitals, mission societies, and other charities.[2]

He ordered his Muslim militias to encircle the American air force base at Incirlik and forced the U.S. military to operate on generated power.[3] *Incirlik Air Base is home to dozens and dozens of American nuclear weapons.*

The Turkish legislature immediately voted him sweeping dictatorial powers, suspended all human rights,[4] and powerful Muslim scholars from

---

[1] http://www.theglobeandmail.com/news/world/Erdoğans-purge-50000-ousted-arrested-or-suspended-inturkey/article30987001/
[2] http://www.huffingtonpost.com/entry/turkey-shuts-schools-charities-emergency_us_57938b99e4b02d5d5ed1d1c4
[3] http://www.latimes.com/world/asia/la-na-turkey-nukes-20160721-snap-story.html
[4] http://www.independent.co.uk/news/world/europe/turkey-coup-attempt-human-rights-president-Erdoğan-purge-turkish-military-a7148166.html

around the world sent Erdoğan an authoritative letter officially naming him the *Mahdi* – the Muslim messiah.[5] [6]

Because of these events, some have speculated that Erdoğan may be something more than just another oppressive dictator…that he could be the evil one long predicted in the Scriptures of Christians and Jews who ushers in the end times and the second coming of Christ.

Is there anything to these claims?

How can we know if we're even in the end times?

Most likely, you're reading this right now because you're wondering if current events are somehow related to biblical prophecy. Does all the upheaval in the news mean the predictions of Revelation are finally coming true?

With every year that passes, it becomes easier and easier to see and understand how the prophecies of old might actually play out. The purpose of this series is to examine current events and lay out the most current understanding of what we might expect in the next decades in light of prophecy — if indeed it *is* time.

Skeptics say that biblical prophecies have been around for thousands of years, so why would they suddenly be coming true now?

Yet, those who say this are actually *fulfilling* prophecy, for the Apostle Peter predicted, *"Above all, you must understand that in the last days scoffers will come, scoffing and following their own evil desires. They will say, "Where is this 'coming' He promised? Ever since our ancestors died, everything goes on as it has since the beginning of creation."* (2 Peter 3:3-4, NIV)

---

[5] http://shoebat.com/2016/07/18/Erdoğan-holding-u-s-tactical-nukes-at-inkirlink-taking-control-of-the-second-most-powerful-army-in-nato-and-is-hailed-as-mahdi/
[6] http://shoebat.com/2017/01/16/major-muslim-leaders-declare-that-within-seven-years-the-muslim-caliphate-will-be-established-and-Erdoğan-will-be-caliph-of-the-muslim-world/

There's a third group of people — those individuals who, unfortunately … just … don't … care. (Since you're reading this, though, chances are you're probably not a member of that group.)

Jesus commanded us, saying, *"And what I say to you, I say to all: Watch!"* (Mark 13:37)

He said this regarding the coming of end time events. Therefore, if you make claim as a follower of Christ, the challenge is for you to obey His command to "Watch," which means you should not only care, but care greatly.

The Purpose of Prophecy

God has dedicated a huge percentage of the Bible to prophecy, *a strong indicator we should care about it.*

Yet, God didn't speak through His prophets simply for the purpose of doing some cheap parlor trick where He predicts the future and then we clap as we see it fulfilled.

True prophecy is essentially *exhortation.* Yes, it does often involve the declaration of events that have not yet happened, but much of what the Old Testament prophets said was simply challenging men and women to change, to submit their lives to the full authority of God.

Therefore, I challenge you to read this series not just to increase your knowledge, but to be transformed. To use the understanding of prophetic events to spur you and those you love into a greater and closer obedience to God.

For as the Book of Revelation says, *"Blessed is he who reads and those who hear the words of this prophecy and keep those things which are written in it; for the time is near."* (Revelation 1:3)

One Minute Please...

BEFORE WE BEGIN, it's essential we discuss *how* to interpret Scripture ... and more specifically, prophecy.

It often seems like everyone and their mother have their own pet methods for interpreting biblical prophecy, but there are rules well-accepted by scholars everywhere, and when we follow them, it's actually not that hard.

Principles to Follow

Principle: *We should always interpret prophetic writing literally when the author meant it to be literal. Also, we shall interpret a thing symbolically when the author clearly meant that thing to be symbolic.*

In spite of what you might think, readers of prophecy can usually know whether something is symbolic or not without much trouble. Frankly, confusion usually enters the picture only when, for whatever reason, we don't like the conclusion we're being drawn to by a passage's clear intent.

For example, Revelation 11 predicts the arrival of Two Witnesses who arrive in Jerusalem and begin preaching powerfully, doing many miracles. Some want to claim Revelation was already fulfilled historically, or they don't want to appeal to the miraculous, so they try to spiritualize this passage by saying the Two Witnesses symbolically represent the Law and the Prophets, or some other similar take, but the passage is clearly describing two literal individuals who will do things that no one has done yet.

On the other hand, Revelation pictures a ten-horned beast that grows to dominate the earth. In this case, Scripture itself tells us that this is a symbolic beast representing a future kingdom, not a literal ten-horned animal wandering around.

Principle: *We will not make assumptions.*

For example, many have struggled with Revelation's references to Babylon as a major player in the end times. For centuries, since modern-day Iraq has continually been seen as a third-world nation, it has required faith to believe it could be a major player in end time events while the globe is dominated by America, Europe, Russia, & China.

Because of this, prophecy teachers typically treat "Babylon" as a code name for Rome (meaning Europe), or for America (the child of Rome, i.e. Europe) or the Catholic Church (Rome).

In support of this, they cite Revelation 17:9 which references the seven hills on which the Whore of Babylon sits. It is *assumed* the symbolic Whore here is the same as Babylon itself, though the rest of the passage indicates they are not the same, but two separate entities.

It is also *assumed* the seven hills are the seven hills of Rome, though many cities have been built on seven hills including Brussels (head of the European Union), Moscow (head of Russia), Tehran (head of Iran), Istanbul (most important city of Turkey and former capital of Rome), and even Mecca and Jerusalem itself!

Therefore, we do well to be alert for assumptions others have made, or even we ourselves may be making. Assumptions can inadvertently prevent us from seeing the right interpretation.

Principle: *We will not make absolute predictions about dates or times. We will not make any* **absolute** *statements regarding our interpretation of prophecy and its relation to current events.*

Want to be publicly be embarrassed and have God prove you wrong? The best way is to start making absolute predictions about how things are exactly going to play out. After all, the Pharisees were prophecy "experts," but somehow they completely missed the references to Jesus's first coming.

REVELATION UNFOLDING

The purpose of this series is simply to lay out what is believed to be the most *probable* scenario(s) based on the best information currently available. Only God knows exactly how everything will play out.

Everything will be clear as day once we've seen it happen, but a *perfect* understanding beforehand is only possible with direct revelation from Him.

Since we know that the Apostle John did receive such a direct Revelation from God, let's start our study by examining what John wrote.

THE BOOK OF REVELATION

JOHN WAS ONE of the twelve disciples chosen by Jesus to carry the message of the Gospel to the world. In the account of Jesus' ministry bearing his name, John described himself as the "disciple that Jesus loved," a humble reference showing a closeness with Jesus shared by few others.

Distinct from that work, the Book of Revelation is John's record of what he saw and heard when God transported him briefly to Heaven to show him what would unfold at the end of time.

The very first verse declares the book is actually the Revelation of Jesus Christ Himself.

When teaching, some prophecy experts have a tendency to jump around in Scripture, pulling single verses from many different books in a disconnected fashion that causes the student to feel like prophecy is an enormous and impossibly complicated puzzle to put together.

Yet, this could not have been God's intent, for He clearly meant for us to understand it.

The Book of Revelation is meant to be interpreted as a *chronological* account of end times' events, and thus it should be read that way. *Chronologically.* In other words, the events of each chapter come after those of the previous.

This writing is not meant to be a commentary on the full Book of Revelation, so we are just going to give a brief overview of the first chapters before digging deeper into Chapter 6 where the apocalyptic events truly begin.

Chapter 1 is a glorious vision of Jesus in Heaven and a description of His majesty. He is seen as the King of Kings and Lord of Lords. From His blazing eyes to His glowing white robes, the description of our Lord is truly powerful and beautiful to the mind.

Chapters 2 and 3 are seven brief letters from Jesus to different churches that existed two thousand years ago in what is now Turkey. Some theologians have speculated that these seven messages also represent the seven different ages of the church during the past two millennia.

We would agree with that assessment, and if those letters are meant to be viewed that way, then we are now living in what would be called the *Laodicean Age*, the final age of the church — the *lukewarm* age.

Chapters 4 and 5 describe a glorious ceremony in Heaven where the Lamb of God (Jesus) takes possession of a special *scroll*.

This scroll is very important. *Everything* that happens in the following chapters is a result of the Lamb of God taking the scroll.

At first, an angel calls out loudly, *"Who is worthy to open the scroll and to loose its seals?"* But, *"no one in heaven or on the earth or under the earth was able to open the scroll, or to look at it."* (Revelation 5:3)

The scroll has writing on both sides, meaning it is full, *complete*, and even all-encompassing in scope — and it is sealed with seven seals. (We'll soon see that the breaking of each one of these seals unleashes a powerful prophetic event.)

So, what kind of all-encompassing document could this be that its very opening launches the end of the world and no one is found worthy to possess it but the Lamb of God Himself?

It has been speculated by theologians that this scroll is essentially the title deed to the Earth — i.e. *a real estate deed* giving ownership of our planet to whoever possesses the document. We agree with that interpretation.

Throughout history, from Alexander the Great, to Caesar, to Napoleon and Hitler, men have tried to take possession of the whole earth, but none have been able, none were worthy.

As Napoleon himself once said, *"I know men; and I tell you that Jesus Christ is no mere man. Between Him and every person in the world there* is no possible term of comparison. Alexander, Caesar, Charlemagne, and I have founded empires. But on what did we rest the creations of our genius? Upon force. Jesus Christ founded His empire upon love; and at this hour millions of men would die for him."

Supporting the idea that the scroll represents a legal deed to the Earth is the vision in Chapter 5 of the saints in Heaven (all believers who have died before us) bowing down to the Lamb of God and singing:

> *You are worthy to take the scroll,*
> *And to open its seals;*
> *For You were slain,*
> *And have redeemed us to God by Your blood*
> *Out of every tribe and tongue and people and nation*

The Lamb of God purchased the Earth with His blood. By taking the scroll, He is taking possession of what is rightfully His, *and only His.*

It is important to note here that the Bible teaches that everything that happens on Earth – from what we see in the news to what happens in your daily life – is merely a reflection of spiritual events in Heaven, including and especially a spiritual war that is ongoing between God's angels and our enemy. (Ephesians 6:12, Daniel 10)

Therefore, while our study of current events and how they might relate to Revelation officially begins with Chapter 6, truly everything begins here in Chapters 4 and 5. The Lamb of God taking possession of His inheritance, the Earth, is the spiritual event that launches everything which follows.

We call it the end of the world … and it truly is the end of the *World* as the Bible defines the "world," meaning the sinful world system run by man under the influence of sin and the enemy. The end of the world means the long-awaited end of corruption and oppression, the end of lust and greed, and the end of murder and abuse.

It is *not*, however, the end of our *life!* Our true life begins once the oppressive world system has finally been destroyed. The Book of Revelation is a vision of how that end comes about.

The Signs

How Can We Know If We're Really in the Last Days?

IF WE'RE GOING to try and connect *current* events to prophecy, we first need to determine if we're even living in the predicted Last Days or not.

The Bible says we will know the end times are upon us when we see all of the following signs coming true at the same time:

- Jews are gathered and return from around the world to live in Israel
- Israel is reborn as a nation
- Strong financial controls (over buying and selling) are possible
- People around the world will be able to witness the same events simultaneously
- The knowledge of many will be increased
- Christians will seek light-hearted teaching that "tickles the ears"
- Christians will be lukewarm
- There will be a great falling away of Christians from the faith
- Men will mock teaching about the end times
- There will be a global increase in all sin
- People will become hard-hearted, unloving
- Men will be possessed by lust
- Sex traffickers will abound (yes, this is predicted specifically)
- There will be a severe increase in violence & sexual sin
- Wars & rumors of war will abound
- Many false Christs and prophets will appear
- There will be a rise in New Age teachings & demonic activity
- Natural disasters will increase greatly
- Earthquakes specifically will increase
- Famine will also increase

- There will be a huge increase in martyred Christians
- The Gospel will be preached to every tribe and nation

For those who keep up with global news, it isn't hard to see that many if not all of these signs have become true today.

Still, some people reading the above list would say, "but there have *always* been natural disasters and wars and lust – these are nothing new, so these signs could happen in any age!" Yet, those who would say such a thing are not being honest.

Take another look. All of these are true today, but what about a hundred years ago? Were *all* of these signs true a century ago?

A hundred years ago, Christians were not lukewarm. There was no great "falling away" from the faith. Instead Christianity was experiencing rapid growth around the world (Africa, China, India). Yet, the Gospel was not even close to being preached to all tribes and nations at that time.

In the 1800's, it was not possible to control the buying and selling of a population on a major scale, nor could people in India witness something happening in Jerusalem as it happened. Nor had Israel been reborn.

Even if one wished to point to some of these signs as having been fulfilled before, the rebirth of Israel, the regathering of the Jews, and the extent of the reach of Christian missionaries are all very measurable and definite events that have never had a true fulfillment before.

And certain signs — like the rebirth of Israel — as we shall see have a maximum limiting factor, meaning that there is a limited period of time after its fulfillment when the last days events can begin.

Let's look at each one of these signs in more detail.

The Sign of the Gathering of Israel

Here, a brief history lesson is required for the uninitiated.

3,000 years ago, King David ruled over all twelve tribes of Israel, and because of his heart for God, God promised David that the Messiah would come from his line of descendants.

Years later, after the death of David's son, Solomon, the ten northern tribes of Israel rebelled, broke off and chose for themselves a new king not descended from David. These northern tribes soon after began straying from God and worshipping idols. Due to their unfaithfulness to God, they were eventually conquered by the Assyrian Empire (Turkey and Northern Iraq) and scattered across the Caucus Mountains and around the Black Sea.

The two southern tribes, Judah and Benjamin, remained in the Promised Land and under the rule of David's descendants. Collectively, these two tribes (along with many from the priestly tribe of Levi) were just called Judah, or the Southern Kingdom of Judah. All Jewish people today are descended from them.

Unfortunately, Judah also eventually rebelled against God, and so God allowed the Babylonian Empire (Southern Iraq) to conquer them 600 years before Christ and to scatter them across its lands. God predicted through the prophets that some Jews would be allowed to return to the land of Judah after 70 years, and they did. The rest who remained behind became the Jewish communities of Iraq, Iran, and the rest of the Middle East.

The Jews who returned to Judah (called *Judaea* or *Iudaea* by the Romans) rebuilt the Temple of God in Jerusalem. Jesus, the long-promised Messiah, lived and ministered among these Jews (the Returned Judah), but they did not recognize Him — again, as predicted by Old Testament prophecy — and He was crucified.

Because of this sin, Judah was once again conquered, this time by the Roman Empire, and scattered across Europe until the 20th century.

Many prophetic passages, especially in the Old Testament, speak of the future *rebirth* of Israel as a nation.

IMPORTANT: We have copies of these documents authoritatively dated by scholars to hundreds of years *before Christ* and *before* the Jewish people were even conquered by the Romans, so for an Old Testament prophet to not only predict the initial scattering, but to accurately predict their return is pretty bold.

> *"Then say to them, Thus says the Lord GOD: 'Surely I will take the children of Israel from among the nations, wherever they have gone, and will gather them from every side and bring them into their own land; and I will make them one nation in the land, on the mountains of Israel...'" (Ezekiel 37:21-22a)*

> *"And I will bring them out from the peoples and gather them from the countries, and will bring them to their own land; I will feed them on the mountains of Israel, in the valleys and in all the inhabited places of the country." (Ezekiel 34:13)*

> *"I will bring back my exiled people Israel; they will rebuild the ruined cities and live in them. They will plant vineyards and drink their wine; they will make gardens and eat their fruit. I will plant Israel in their own land, never again to be uprooted from the land I have given them," says the Lord your God." (Amos 9:14-15, NLT)*

> *"I will be found by you," says the* LORD. *"I will end your captivity and restore your fortunes. I will gather you out of the nations where I sent you and will bring you home again to your own land." (Jeremiah 29:14)*

> *"It shall come to pass in that day that the Lord shall set His hand again the **second time** to recover the remnant of His people who are left, from Assyria* [Turkey & Northern Iraq] *and Egypt* [Lower Egypt], *from Pathros* [Upper Egypt] *and Cush* [Ethiopia & Sudan], *from Elam* [Iran] *and Shinar* [Northern Syria], *from Hamath* [Southern Syria] *and the islands of the sea* [Europe]. *He will set up a banner for the nations, and will assemble the outcasts of*

Israel, and gather together the dispersed of Judah from the four corners of the earth." (Isaiah 11:11-12)

"Lift up your eyes all around, and see: they all gather together, they come to you; your sons shall come from afar, and your daughters shall be nursed at your side. Then you shall see and become radiant, and your heart shall swell with joy; because the abundance of the sea shall be turned to you, the wealth of the Gentiles shall come to you." (Isaiah 60:4-5)

God is now fulfilling these prophecies! Of the estimated 14 million Jews in the world today, a little over half of them are now in Israel. Before the 20th century, almost none were.

All of the nations of the earth today, with the exception of the United States, have been virtually emptied of their Jewish populations. Only the United States still has a significant Jewish population left, and with more than 5 million Jews living there, together with Israel the two nations host 83% of the world's Jewish population.

In other words, the prophecies about the regathering are now clearly coming true.

ZACK MASON

The Sign of the Rebirth of the Nation of Israel

On May 14th, 1948, a nation – the Nation of Israel – came into existence in a single day.

Think about the significance of that! In the history of the world, what other ethnic group has ever been scattered across the earth into all the nations, yet retained its distinct genetic and cultural identity without mixing with surrounding peoples *for not just centuries, but millennia,* and then returned 2,500 years later to the land of its origin to be reborn as a nation?

The answer is: None. This has *never* happened before. Only Israel.

Imagine Russia conquering Scotland and completely annihilating or exiling all Scottish people and replacing them with Russians. Then, in the year 4,000 AD, all the Scots scattered throughout the world, who have somehow retained their distinct culture and identity as a people group, return to Scotland, rebuild the nation of William Wallace and Robert the Bruce, and reinstitute an extinct Gaelic as their national language.

Such a thing is crazy to consider. And the Scots currently scattered in the U.S., Canada, and Australia haven't even maintained their cultural identity over 200 years, much less 2,000.

Yet, the Jewish people have done all that, and they did reinstitute Hebrew as the national language (which until then had been a dead language).

Not only that, but the prophet Ezekiel predicted that Israel would be reborn exactly 907,200 days after the end of the Babylonian Captivity in 536 BC[7]. That number of days was completed exactly on the 14th of May, 1948, the day Israel was declared and recognized as a nation!

Importantly for us, Jesus said, *"Now learn this parable from the fig tree: When its branch has already become tender and puts forth leaves, you know that summer is near. So you also, when you see all these things, know that it is near—at the doors! Assuredly, I say to you, this generation will by no means pass away till all these things take place."* (Matthew 24:32-34)

---

[7] http://www.grantjeffrey.com/pdf/JeffBIBLE-EzekVision2.pdf

The fig tree is *always* a symbol for Israel in Scripture.[8] So, Jesus' reference is very intentional and what He is essentially saying is that when we see Israel blooming again, we will know the end has arrived – that the generation that witnesses the blooming of Israel will not pass away until these things have begun to pass.

There does remain a question as to how long this "generation" is considered to be. Some say 40 years, others 80 or 120. However, what's clearly *not* possible is that it be longer than 120 as that is the maximum life span of a man.

While the Rebirth of Israel predicted by Ezekiel is clearly connected to 1948, there is still a question as to what event exactly corresponds to the fig tree blooming predicted by Jesus in Matthew? Is it also referencing the establishment of Israel in 1948? Or did the clock start ticking when Israel reconquered Jerusalem in 1967? Or is it instead more spiritual in nature, referring to the spiritual revival occurring among the Orthodox Jews right now? (Thousands are currently coming to believe in Jesus as the Jewish Messiah and this movement is accelerating.)

Yet, I would point out the blooming of a tree is not a fixed event. It is a process. Therefore, it is probable that all of these things represent the process of the Blooming of Israel. It has not yet finished solidifying its national borders and the spiritual revival has just begun.

Regardless, it seems our generation *is* likely the generation that will see these things begin to pass.

---

[8] https://www.factsaboutisrael.uk/israel-fig-tree/

The Sign of Strong Financial Control

Everyone has heard of the "mark of the beast." This is perhaps the best-known prophecy of all regarding the end of days.

> *"He causes all, both small and great, rich and poor, free and slave, to receive a mark on their right hand or on their foreheads, and that no one may buy or sell except one who has the mark or the name of the beast, or the number of his name." (Revelation 13:16-17)*

So, yes, the Book of Revelation clearly says the antichrist will require people to take a special mark representing his name, and that without that mark no one will be able to buy and sell.

Let's consider this possible fulfillment in past generations. Could such a thing have been possible during the Roman Empire? No.

How about during the 1800's? Or even after World War II?

Sure, it's always been possible for a dictator to issue an edict making it illegal for people to buy and sell without his mark, but it was never possible for them to *actually* control it so absolutely in the sense that Revelation seems to convey.

Not until modern times that is.

Actually, not until very *recent*, modern times.

Cash is not controllable. You can pass laws restricting what you can buy and sell and who can buy and sell, but, as we all know, that certainly hasn't stopped the illegal drug trade. Or the exploitation of women for sex.

Governments know that only a cashless society is truly controllable. Only when money is electronic and all transactions must be done through government-controlled bank accounts, is full control possible.

The United States and Europe have been growing increasingly cashless for decades, but it is only recently that much of the rest of the world has had the banking and financial infrastructure to follow suit. Only *very* recently are many third world countries fully entering the realm of digital money.

As the use of mobile phones for payments increases, this will further solidify.

On a mission trip to Kenya a few years ago, I saw this personally as banks' main advertising was oriented around mobile phone payments and getting Kenyans to join the program. And I saw that even the poorest Kenyans, the Maasai, had cell phones and could participate.

Bottom line: Financial control, as it's described in Revelation 13, was not possible in history, but today it is.

The Sign of Global Communications

"Then those from the peoples, tribes, tongues, and nations will see their dead bodies three-and-a-half days…" (Revelation 11:9)

The above verse is referring to the antichrist's murder of God's two witnesses in Jerusalem (the two witnesses are described in Chapter 11). The language indicates people from all around the world will "see" their dead bodies, and there are other events in Revelation that use similar language.

Only today in an age of global mass media was it possible for this prophecy to be truly fulfilled. Years ago, I was visiting remote places in Bangladesh to share the good news of Christ with poor villagers. As I entered mud hut after mud hut, something struck me: every single one of those villagers had a television. They had mud floors, crude furniture and no other amenities to speak of, but just about every one of them had a flat-screen TV.

Consider how bold John must have been to make such a prophecy 2,000 years ago. Claiming that everyone in the world would be able to see their bodies over three and a half days when travel time just to Rome meant weeks if not months? He had no concept of what technology would be some day. It would have been impossible to conceive. Even a hundred years ago, it was not possible for people of all nations to witness something together. Back then, it was thought that somehow God would supernaturally allow everyone to see the bodies.

Today, if an event as significant as the murder of God's two prophets in the streets of Jerusalem were to occur, we would *all* see these things unfolding live on our television sets, computers, tablets, or phones.

Only in modern times is it possible for the prophecy of Revelation 11:9 to be fulfilled.

The Sign of Knowledge and Travel

"...even to the time of the end: many shall run to and fro, and knowledge shall be increased." (Daniel 12:4)

We don't really need to point out how much scientific and technological advancement has occurred in the last one hundred years. The question is: Was it equally possible to say this prophecy had been fulfilled in previous centuries?

During the Middle Ages, it would have been a far stretch to claim that knowledge had increased, though clearly there were a few advancements. But certainly, people didn't "run to and fro." They were fairly locked into living where they were born.

During the 17th and 18th centuries we would have said the same thing. In the 1800's we do start to see a good bit of scientific knowledge achieved, but men still didn't "run to and fro." Agriculture dominated and men were still married to their farms.

Really, it was only starting in the late 20th century that we see such a dramatic increase in scientific knowledge and technology combined with a hectic pace of life.

Today, men and women truly run about "to and fro," and not just in the United States. Rush hour traffic is now a global phenomenon. Businessmen and women fly across the world for single meetings before returning home (at least before Coronavirus).

And of course, knowledge continues to accelerate.

This prophecy is now fulfilled.

The Sign of Teaching that Tickles the Ears

Referring to the last days, Paul says in 2 Timothy:

> *"For the time will come when they will not endure sound doctrine; but after their own lusts shall they heap to themselves teachers, having itching ears; And they shall turn away their ears from the truth, and shall be turned unto fables." (2 Timothy 4:3-4)*

This prediction says that in the end times, people will turn away from biblical truth and embrace teaching that tickles their ears and enables their "lusts." That not only covers sexual lust, but also greed and coveting. It also says people will "be turned unto fables."

A little over one hundred years ago, Charles Darwin developed the Theory of Evolution, a pseudo-scientific fable designed to rid men of the authority of God over them. True, *honest* science has actually proven the Theory of Evolution false, and with overwhelming evidence.[9][10][11] (Please understand that *adaptation*, otherwise known as microevolution, i.e. changes within a single species, has indeed been observed and validated, but macro-evolution, the idea of one species evolving into another, has been nullified.)

The Fable of Evolution was not originally embraced by scientists, but by rebellious individuals interested in denying God. With the passage of time, these rebels used deception and intentional power grabs to dominate the scientific community until very few peer-reviewed papers that argued against the theory could get published.

Man rejects God out of a determination to not be ruled by Him. Of course, once he has done that, there is no longer any governor on morality. And we're all seeing the results of that throughout every level of society today.

Unfortunately, this rejection of God's sovereignty has deeply infected the Church as well. In previous generations, American Christians read books

---

[9] Behe, Michael J., *Darwin's Black Box,* Free Press, 2006
[10] Perloff, James, *Tornado in a Junkyard*, Refuge Books, 1999
[11] Meyer, Stephen C., *Darwin's Doubt*, HarperOne, 2014

like "The Calvary Road" and "My Utmost for His Highest," books that call for a sacrifice of oneself to obey and worship God and love others.

Today, we worship ourselves by reading things like "Your Best Life Now" by Joel Osteen which reorients the Gospel to having a focus of blessing our lives rather than provoking a submission to God and repentance, or "Good Christian Sex" whose author claims that God really doesn't mind us having sex outside of marriage, or "God and the Gay Christian" by Matthew Vines which argues the Bible doesn't say homosexuality is a sin.

Some popular Christian pastors have even begun to teach there is no such thing as hell, that everyone is going to Heaven no matter what (what about Hitler?). Truly, these and other teachings deny the power of God and are spoken to tickle the ears, to gain fans and influence, and enable people's lusts.

Has this prophecy been fulfilled before in previous ages? No.

Only recently have the people fully embraced fables and teaching that tickles their ears.

(It is interesting to note the Bible says they *"shall they heap to themselves teachers"* to enable their lusts, so it is the people driving this, not the teachers, but that is another book!)

The Sign of Lukewarm Christians

As we said earlier, Jesus' letters to the seven churches represent the seven different ages of the church. Therefore, as the letter to the church in Laodicea is the last of the seven letters, it represents Jesus' message for churches in the last part of history.

Here is what Jesus has to say:

> *"I know your works, that you are neither cold nor hot. I could wish you were cold or hot. So then, because you are lukewarm, and neither cold nor hot, I will vomit you out of My mouth. Because you say, 'I am rich, have become wealthy, and have need of nothing' and do not know that you are wretched, miserable, poor, blind, and naked..."*
> *(Revelation 3:15-17)*

This is not good. The last church age will be lukewarm and Jesus has nothing but scathing words for them.

So, is this true of us today, or not?

Anyone who is part of the American church today is forced to admit that, as a whole, we are indeed very lukewarm. Americans don't *hate* God. On the contrary, we all profess a great *affection* for Him. But we have no passion.

In general, we no longer give to Him sacrificially of our time or money. Instead, we live as we see fit, half-heartedly seeking God's blessing on what we want to do and throwing the occasional spare change at Kingdom work.

This is also true of Canada, Europe, Australia, Latin America, and every other Christian culture that is not currently experiencing persecution.

We are neither hot nor cold, and so this prophecy is also fulfilled.

The Sign of the Great Falling Away

"Let no one deceive you by any means; for that Day will not come unless the falling away comes first..." (2 Thessalonians 2:3)

Beyond growing tepid in their faith, the Bible says that many Christians will renounce their faith. ***This has been expected for centuries and is called the Great Falling Away.***

Over the past two decades, the number of Americans who profess a certainty in their belief in God has been dropping by 7% - 9% every seven years. That number is now down so low that only 63% of Americans are sure there is a God. The number of Americans who have declared themselves to have no religion at all has shot up to 23%.[12]

Daily prayer is dropping. Regular Bible reading is on the decrease. Church attendance is falling dramatically. Statistics in America are the most readily available, but it is well-known that the current trends here are also happening in Latin America and Canada and that Europe began its "falling away" from the faith of its ancestors decades ago.

According to the Bible, this falling away is only going to increase and accelerate as we move further into the last days.

This poses a very difficult obstacle for many who would believe. When the perception around you is that Christianity is losing its influence, that society is turning its back on faith, it requires greater conviction not to be deceived and continue to go against the flow.

What needs to be remembered is that the Bible warned you about this day thousands of years ago, saying "let no one deceive you!" The falling away must happen, but you will not be excused of your responsibility before God based on what the rest of society believes.

You are responsible regardless.

---

[12] http://www.pewforum.org/2015/11/03/u-s-public-becoming-less-religious/

The Sign of Mocking

In his second letter, Peter said:

> *"Knowing this first: that scoffers will come in the last days, walking according to their own lusts, and saying, "Where is the promise of His coming? For since the fathers fell asleep, all things continue as they were from the beginning of creation." (2 Peter 3:3-4)*

This is an easy one for you to test. Just start asking your friends and neighbors what they think about Jesus' second coming. Do they think He could come soon? The most common response you are most likely to receive is "People have been saying it was the end of the world for thousands of years, why is today any different?"

Truly, this was not a common sentiment a hundred years ago, but since you and I weren't living back then, it is hard to *prove* people didn't say that. Nevertheless, the fact that the majority of the people you know *would* respond that way today makes this prophecy currently true.

It is one more sign that we are living in the last days.

The Sign of Global Increase in Sin

In Matthew 24, Jesus said:

> *"and because iniquity shall abound, the love of many shall wax cold."*

Do we really have to prove this one? Are people more or less sinful (according to biblical standards) than they were a hundred years ago, or even fifty years ago?

Divorce and adultery are rampant. Websites and apps have been developed to help people cheat on their spouses. Swinger parties (orgies) are now becoming more mainstream. Men visit places like Hooters with their wives without shame, are addicted to pornography, and sleep with prostitutes at alarming rates. Teenage and college girls have become promiscuous, providing oral sex at times with the flippancy of a hug, and letting boys do shameful things to them in public at Spring Break getaways.

Homosexuality, transvestitism, child molestation, and bestiality are all on the rise. The first two are now being normalized and the normalization of the third is now being called for by the elitists since so many government officials are tired of hiding their own pedophilia.

Theft and corruption have infiltrated every level of the government of every country, including the United States. No nation can claim to have a truly honest justice system at this point.

Greed, coveting, and materialism have gripped the hearts of men everywhere, igniting class warfare on a powerful scale.

Slavery has resurged across the globe and threatens the freedom of people everywhere. Democracy is being mocked through voter fraud. Prisons are overflowing, yet violent prisoners are being freed for political reasons.

Truly, sin is abounding.

The Sign of Love Growing Cold

"...the love of many shall wax cold." (Matthew 24:12)

Jesus said the result of the increase in sin would be an increased apathy by people toward the welfare of others.

In fact, today studies show that the upcoming generation of millennials is seriously lacking in empathy, i.e. concern, for others.[13] Studies also show upcoming generations are generally more narcissistic.

Business leaders often cite statistics showing that millennials tend to throw their purchasing power behind companies that they believe are funding a good social cause with their profits.

However, this trend can be deceptive. Some claim a hidden reason behind the trend is that millennials are subconsciously trying to make up for their lack of personal sacrifice for others and ease their conscience by buying things from "good" companies.

On the other hand, the donation of time and money in a sacrificial way by this younger generation is on the decline.

This is natural, of course.

Today's young people have suffered from the overabundant divorce, adultery, sex abuse, greed and materialism of their parents. As a result, they've lost trust.

If they couldn't trust their parents to not hurt them, their survival-oriented, toughened hearts can't trust others either, or serve them sacrificially (agape love). They have to be healed by the Great Physician first.

---

[13] http://www.scientificamerican.com/article/what-me-care/

But this is not just a problem of Millennials. Truly the love of many has grown cold not just across America, but around the world. Apathy is a growing plague.[14]

Decades ago, small town life dominated the America landscape. You knew your neighbors, you slept with the doors unlocked, and if someone's barn burned down, those same neighbors would be right there to help you rebuild.

Today, no one knows their neighbors. We saturate our days envying people on social media we haven't seen for years and are so desperate to keep up with the Joneses in every way that we don't have time to visit someone in the hospital when they fall sick.

Timmy's got soccer…on Friday we have the awards ceremony…Saturday's the only day we have together as a family, so we need to protect that time…etc.

In the 1980's, when famine was devastating Ethiopia, the American people, entertainers, and politicians rallied together to raise millions to send help. But when the communist Ethiopian government let the food sit at the docks and rot instead of distributing it and took the money to fund a military machine that crushed its opponents, our love grew a little colder.

Decades later, when the tidal wave hit Indonesia and Hurricane Katrina slammed New Orleans, people showed up generously again, though with dimmed enthusiasm. After all, natural disasters were on the increase and it was becoming wearying.

When the Clinton Foundation and the Red Cross took in together close to a $1 billion in donations to help rebuild Haiti after the 2010 earthquake but failed to actually send any of it to Haiti, we grew even more skeptical and reluctant to give.

When the Islamic State and others massacred Middle Eastern Christians by the thousands, more of us just shrugged our shoulders and said, "We're not the world's police force."

---

[14] http://thelantern.com/2013/05/commentary-apathy-in-america-is-a-growing-plague/

And now as I write this, families around the world have been in isolation for months due to coronavirus lockdowns. Generally, many people's mental health has suffered as a result, and studies show that isolation is a cause of reduced empathy, increased apathy.[15] Social distancing has the same effect.

Walking around with masks covering our smiles, people are afraid to hug or even shake hands. Some have begun to view others as a potential enemy carrying a virus that could kill them.

Regardless of how you might feel about these things, the sign has clearly come true. We are hardened and our love has grown colder.

---

[15] https://www.scientificamerican.com/article/what-me-care/

The Sign of Men Possessed by Lust

> *"...how they told you that there would be mockers in the last time who would walk according to their own ungodly lusts." (Jude 1:18)*

Lust has grown to plague levels in America and across the world. In this digital age, pornography's addiction and influence continue to rise at alarming levels.

According to the Barna Group[16], 57% of young adults seek out porn on a daily, weekly, or monthly basis. Considering that this 57% is of *all* young people (in other words it includes young adult *females)*, then that statistic represents a *huge* number of young adult males.

More shockingly, 56% of young adults and teens view a failure to recycle as morally wrong, *but only 32% of the same group feels it's morally wrong to look at porn.* That means that almost *twice* as many young people find recycling offenses to be worse than pornography.

Combine that with the fact that the majority of Americans don't believe images displaying full nudity even constitute porn,[17] and you've got a very, very low percentage of Americans who feel it's wrong to lust after naked images of a person.

It is a sad state when almost two-thirds of us think it's damnable to throw away a plastic bottle, but over 80% of us think that to engage lust with a photographic image acquired by exploiting someone sexually is at least neutral morally or maybe even somehow contributing to society.

So, once more, the question arises: what about the timing of this? Is this something that has always been true?

No, it is only true now in the digital age.

---

[16] http://www.barna.com/research/porn-in-the-digital-age-new-research-reveals-10-trends/#.V8SFdzWKIg4
[17] http://www.barna.com/the-porn-phenomenon/#.V8SEkTWKIg4

Previous generations hated pornography and condemned it. The fact of the change is seen once again in the statistics. While only 32% of *young adults* say viewing porn is wrong, 54% of adults over 25 do say it is wrong.[18] This is a clear generational difference and once again is the fulfillment of a biblical sign of the end times.

---

[18] http://www.barna.com/research/porn-in-the-digital-age-new-research-reveals-10-trends/#.V8SFdzWKIg4

The Sign of Sex Trafficking

Within a famous passage regarding the nature of men in the last days, the Bible says:

> *"For of this sort are those who creep into households and make captives of gullible women loaded down with sins, led away by various lusts ..." (2 Timothy 3:6-7)*

In Ellicott's Commentary on these verses[19], the author says:

"The Greek word [often] translated "make captive" is a peculiar one and is only found in comparatively later Greek. It is supposed to be a word of Alexandrian or Macedonian origin. It here represents these women as wholly under the influence of these bad men, to the utter destruction of all true, healthy, home life."

Some see the phrases "loaded down with sins" and "led away by various lusts" as referring to the women, but the Greek lends itself to another possibility that these phrases refer to the men who are taking captive the women.

The most literal translation would be, *"Out of this type are those who creep into households and take prisoners of vulnerable women, sin-burdened, various lusts-driven ..."* The verbs in those phrases are in the accusative neuter case, not the feminine. Thus, they can apply to either the men or the women.

Regardless, what do you call it when men sneak into lives and take prisoner vulnerable women? What else but sexual exploitation or sex trafficking?

It is a no brainer that any man taking prisoner a vulnerable woman is by definition loaded with sin and driven by various lusts of both sex and money.

---

[19] http://biblehub.com/commentaries/2_timothy/3-6.htm

2 Timothy seems to say that sex trafficking will abound in the last days. It is commonly known that sex trafficking has exploded across the globe in recent years in every country.

This makes one more sign that is now fulfilled which had not been true previously.

The Sign of Violence & Homosexuality

> *"...But as the days of Noah were, so shall also the coming of the Son of Man be." (Matthew 24:37)*

> *"Likewise also as it was in the days of Lot; they did eat, they drank, they bought, they sold, they planted, they built; But the same day that Lot went out of Sodom it rained fire and brimstone from heaven, and destroyed them all. Even thus shall it be in the day when the Son of Man is revealed." (Luke 17:28-30)*

Regarding the days of Noah, God says, *"The earth also was corrupt before God, and the earth was filled with violence." (Genesis 6:11)*

The same was true with Sodom and Gomorrah. The people of Sodom were not just guilty of sexual sins like homosexuality, but they were violent. The men of these towns were so filled with lust and violence that they raped and murdered any visitors to the town they could find, regardless of sex.

And so God judged them.

Both homosexuality and violence are indeed on a severe increase in the United States and around the world. We're all aware of the rise of the homosexual movement. Gay marriage is now legal in many countries, and homosexuals are now beginning to use the power of government to persecute traditional Christians.[20] [21] [22] [23] [24]

---

[20] https://www.crisismagazine.com/2013/gay-persecution-of-christians-the-latest-evidence
[21] https://www.dailywire.com/news/targeted-christian-baker-sued-again-this-time-over-transgender-cake
[22] https://www.christianpost.com/news/church-sued-for-2-3-million-for-not-hosting-lgbt-event-in-building-it-owns.html
[23] https://pjmedia.com/faith/tyler-o-neil/2017/02/23/lgbt-group-announces-plan-to-invade-church-space-in-ohio-n97434
[24] https://hnewswire.com/lgbt-is-out-to-destroy-christianity/

Contrary to the wishful thinking of many, the facts are in and global violence has increased strongly over past decades.[25] [26] Statistics show this increase is not due solely to violence by the Islamic State or other terrorists either, but that violence in every category is up across the world, from murder rates to violent protests.

However, something that isn't talked about as much is the fact that unrestrained homosexual communities typically descend into the most violent of cultures.[27] This isn't just the opinion of this author either, but the official determination of the CDC.[28] Truly, the violence of Sodom and Gomorrah was not unique to their cities but is actually the standard outcome for any community that gives itself over to homosexuality.

Regardless, we must ask whether this sign is coming true today?

The answer of course is a resounding yes. Both homosexuality and violence are growing rapidly.

---

[25] http://blogs.reuters.com/great-debate/2015/03/20/breaking-a-decades-long-trend-the-world-gets-more-violent/
[26] http://www.telegraph.co.uk/news/worldnews/big-question-kcl/11711266/Mapped-How-the-world-became-more-violent.html
[27] https://www.buzzfeed.com/dominicholden/most-lgbt-people-in-san-francisco-experience-violence-study?utm_term=.jiOgEk2wVy#.epO0dXAY6z
[28] http://www.onenewsnow.com/culture/2015/12/13/cdc-report-homosexual-lifestyle-extremely-violent

The Sign of Wars and Rumors of Wars

> *"... And ye shall hear of wars and rumors of wars ... For nation shall rise against nation and kingdom against kingdom." (Matthew 24:6-7)*

A landmark study out of the University of Warwick[29] has revealed an alarming growth in the number of wars (defined as "pairwise conflicts") since 1870. Yet, the study shows not just a simple increase in armed conflict and tension, but a clear ongoing acceleration.

Before World War I, the number of conflicts grew by an average of 6% per year, but *between* World War I and II, the rate jumped to 17% growth per year.

Still, that was just a violent time. After World War II, we had a time of relative peace, right?

Wrong. During the Cold War, the number of global wars increased by 31% each year, and the number of wars only accelerated further after that. (After the Soviet Union fell in 1991, the number of pairwise conflicts grew by an alarming 36% per year.)

Then, with the Arab Spring, conflicts in Sudan and Yemen, massacres in Nigeria, famine in Venezuela, the fight against ISIS, a severe militaristic build-up in China, and now even violent protests inside the United States, there is no peace on the horizon.

One can blame arms dealers and the proliferation of cheap weaponry or whatever cause we wish to identify thinking that somehow explains the phenomenon – but it doesn't matter if you can *explain* the phenomenon. Jesus didn't say the wars and rumors of wars would have no human explanation – he didn't require them to be supernaturally inspired – He

---

[29] https://warwick.ac.uk/newsandevents/pressreleases/wars_steadily_increase/

simply predicted them and told us when we saw the rise in war to know that we were near the end.

Here is a list of major current conflicts in the world in which more than 1,000 people have been killed in recent years[30]:

- War in Afghanistan
- Iraqi Civil War
- Boko Haram Insurgency
- Syrian Civil War
- Kurdish-Turkish Conflict
- Somali Civil War
- War in North-West Pakistan
- Mexican Drug War
- Libyan Civil War
- Yemeni Civil War
- Sinai Insurgency
- South Kordofan Conflict
- South Sudanese Civil War
- War in Donbass

Beyond those, there are *additionally* dozens of active armed conflicts where between 100 and 1,000 people have been killed in the last three years[31] - and we have not yet begun to discuss the *rumors* of war.

It is curious that Jesus would make such a distinction between wars and *rumors* of war, but He did. He said that a sign of the end would be an overabundance of threatened or potential wars between nations.

This author has been following current events for many years, and never before has the world seemed like such a powder keg as it is today. Keep in mind that even during the Cold War when the threat of war was so

---

[30] https://en.wikipedia.org/wiki/List_of_ongoing_armed_conflicts
[31] https://en.wikipedia.org/wiki/List_of_ongoing_armed_conflicts

prevalent, the threat back then was only of *a single* rumor of war, a feared conflict between the U.S. and the Soviet Union. In contrast, today, those threats and rumors fly around like confetti at an arms dealer parade.

Think about the rumblings that have been circulating through global news lately. Below is a *partial* list (and by the time this writing hits the presses, some of these rumors may have blossomed into actual armed conflict).

- China is threatening war against Taiwan[32]
- China is threatening a "cold war" with the United States[33]
- China is threatening Australia with economic war[34]
- China and Russia threatened Japan for maintaining its maritime rights[35]
- China has threatened India with a "large-scaled conflict" over a border dispute and one small battle has already erupted.[36]
- Tensions are building between Japan and South Korea[37]
- North Korea is threatening to reignite the war with South Korea[38]
- North Korea is threatening a nuclear attack on the United States[39]
- Russia has threatened the United States with a "massive response" if the U.S. deploys certain weapons on submarines.[40]

---

[32] https://www.thetimes.co.uk/article/china-threatens-to-smash-taiwan-and-force-reunification-xb3kdjz5l
[33] https://www.voanews.com/east-asia-pacific/voa-news-china/china-warns-us-brink-starting-new-cold-war-beijing
[34] https://www.dailymail.co.uk/news/article-8353231/China-warns-Australia-feel-pain-economic-punishment.html
[35] https://www.express.co.uk/news/world/910938/china-japan-south-china-sea-russia-vladimir-putin-us-senkaku-islands-diaoyu-islands
[36] https://www.express.co.uk/news/world/1299518/world-war-3-china-news-india-latest-conflict-border-LAC-Galwan-Valley-xi-jinping-modi
[37] https://www.nytimes.com/2019/08/04/world/asia/japan-south-korea-feud.html
[38] https://nypost.com/2020/06/23/north-korea-threatens-new-round-of-the-korean-war-to-end-us-report/
[39] https://www.usnews.com/news/world-report/articles/2020-06-26/north-korea-threatens-us-with-nuclear-attack
[40] https://www.voanews.com/europe/russia-threatens-massive-response-if-us-deploys-low-yield-nukes-subs

- Russia is threatening to ignite a civil war in Ukraine.[41]
- Pakistan is threatening India with war over Kashmir.[42]

It is important to note that the above are just recent headlines regarding the world's *major* nations – and we haven't even mentioned the threats against Israel.

Here's a fun game: Google the terms "war" and "threaten" along with any nation of your choice, especially in Asia. See what comes up.

Never before in history have so many significant countries been so belligerent against each other at the same time. Also, importantly, *every single nuclear power, except for France, is now involved in very serious threats of all-out war.*

We do indeed live in interesting times.

---

[41] https://www.thedailybeast.com/cheats/2014/04/08/russia-threatens-ukraine-civil-war
[42] https://www.businessinsider.com/pakistan-india-threat-war-kashmir-2019-9

The Sign of False Christs

"... many shall come in My Name, saying, I am Christ ... and many false prophets shall arise and deceive many." (Matthew 24:4-5,11)

Admittedly, this sign seems to be the last to come to pass. While it is easy to see violence and other major signs staring us in the face from our TV screens on a daily basis, this author has personally not encountered anyone who has claimed to be Jesus.

Yet, there are indeed a number of individuals around the world who claim to be the reincarnated Jesus. Charisma News has an excellent article on the subject which documents some of the latest claimants.[43] A complete list of these cult leaders exists on Wikipedia.[44]

In the 19th century, there were just a handful of individuals who claimed to be Christ. That number grew dramatically in the 20th century to several dozen, and so far another six have come forward in the 21st century.

These numbers don't necessarily seem large enough to fulfill Jesus' prediction yet, especially since the number of followers is still relatively small. Yet, we do see a clear, marked increase.

It's a painful thing to see people have become so corrupt and arrogant that they would claim to be Jesus Himself, but this sign may now be coming to pass.

If we are indeed in the last days, the number of claimants and their followers will continue to grow.

---

[43] http://www.charismanews.com/opinion/watchman-on-the-wall/40277-many-false-christs-are-rising-but-maybe-not-like-we-thought
[44] https://en.wikipedia.org/wiki/List_of_people_claimed_to_be_Jesus

The Sign of New Age Teachings

"... Now the Spirit expressly says that in latter times some will depart from the faith, giving heed to deceiving spirits and doctrines of demons ..." (1 Timothy 4:1)

Today, it is no stretch to say that two of the most influent spiritual teachers in the United States are Oprah Winfrey and Joel Osteen, and Oprah has done more than anyone to take the New Age religion mainstream.

New Age teaching is characterized by a rejection of the Bible as the authoritative Word of God, by a rejection of Christ as the *only* Way to salvation, by a belief that the physical universe itself is God, and by a belief that as we recognize we are one with the universe (and that the power of God lies within us), we can become our own gods, controlling our destiny.

This is the complete opposite of all biblical teaching. The Bible teaches that the universe was created by God and is subject to His will, that we are helpless without Him, and that the *only* Way to salvation is through forgiveness for our rebellion through the merciful, atoning work of Jesus Christ.[45]

Joel Osteen is different from Oprah. He is a highly encouraging and positive pastor who leads the largest church in the United States. Unfortunately, he has also slipped into a subtle failure to preach the Gospel and instead replaced it with a Prosperity Gospel that teaches that wealth and health are the end goals of life. This style teaching also relegates God to be the fulfiller of our wishes rather than the Savior of our souls. Here are a few quotes from Osteen.

Osteen: *"God wants us to have healthy, positive self-images, to see ourselves as priceless treasures. He wants us to feel good about*

---

[45] https://www.lifesitenews.com/news/the-worlds-most-dangerous-spiritual-guru-oprah-begins-10-week-online-new-ag

ourselves... God sees you as a champion... He regards you as a strong, courageous, successful, overcoming person"

These are partial truths, which makes the whole all the more deceptive. God *does* love us and wants the best for us, but whether or not we have positive images of ourselves should be determined solely by our position in Him. We should *not* have positive images of ourselves if we are simultaneously embracing sin, rather we should humbly fear God and walk with Him in submissive obedience.

Osteen: "Whatever your mountain is, you must do more than think about it, more than pray about it; you must speak to that obstacle... Start calling yourself healed, happy, whole, blessed, and prosperous. Stop talking to God about how big your mountains are and start talking to your mountains about how big your God is."

On the surface, it's tempting to read this with a positive interpretation as if it's just calling us to have greater faith, but truly this teaching is over the top. There is *no* value in speaking to inanimate obstacles. We should always appeal to our Father in Heaven. Osteen is switching God's role as a Father who cares for us to that of a servant who is always standing by waiting to remove the obstacles in our way as we desire.[46]

And then we have newly fallen prophets like Rob Bell. Until recently, Bell was a respected Christian teacher. However, he published a book that has become his *opus magnum*, "Love Wins." In this book, he reveals that he has come to believe in Universalism – the belief that *everyone* will eventually go to Heaven, that *no one* will suffer hell for eternity.[47] His stated reason for adopting this belief was to not turn anyone off from the Gospel.

In *Love Wins*, Bell says, "What Jesus does is declare that He, and He alone, is saving everybody. And then He leaves the door way, way open."[48]

---

[46] http://beginningandend.com/prosperity-gospel-wild-joel-osteen-myles-munroe-charging-100-services/
[47] http://www.goodfight.org/a_t_rob_bell.html
[48] http://www.goodfight.org/a_t_rob_bell.html

Yet, what Jesus actually said was:

> "...For wide is the gate and broad is the way that leads to destruction, and there are many who go in by it. Because narrow is the gate and difficult is the way which leads to life, and there are few who find it." (Matthew 7:13, NKJV)

Bell also says, "Forgiveness is unilateral. God isn't waiting for us to get it together, to clean up, shape up, get up—God has already done it." (p. 189)

And yet, God has said through the prophet Ezekiel:

> "And you have encouraged the wicked by promising them life, even though they continue in their sins." (Ezekiel 13:22b, NLT)

> "Son of man, I have made you a watchman for the people of Israel; so hear the word I speak and give them warning from me. When I say to the wicked, 'You wicked person, you will surely die,' and you do not speak out to dissuade them from their ways, that wicked person will die for their sin, and I will hold you accountable for their blood." (Ezekiel 33:7-8, NIV)

Rob Bell should truly tremble for the blood of many will be on his hands.

The New Age movement, the Prosperity Gospel, and Universalism are all teachings of demons who whisper these lies into their false prophets' ears.

Unfortunately, one has to recognize that this sin is also coming to pass today, that more and more false teachers preach such things in order to easily gain more followers, or to achieve wealth themselves.

Jesus said, *"Whoever believes in the Son has eternal life, but whoever rejects the Son will not see life, for God's wrath remains on them." (John 3:36, NIV)*

> "Then they will call on me, but I will not answer; they will seek me diligently, but they will not find me. Because they hated knowledge and did not choose the fear of the LORD" (Proverbs 1:28-29)

REVELATION UNFOLDING

The Sign of Natural Disasters

"And there will be great earthquakes in various places ... and there will be fearful sights and great signs from heaven .... and upon the earth distress of nations, with perplexity; the sea and the waves roaring; Men's hearts failing them for fear, and for looking after those things which are coming on the earth: for the powers of heaven shall be shaken."
(Luke 21:11, 25-26)

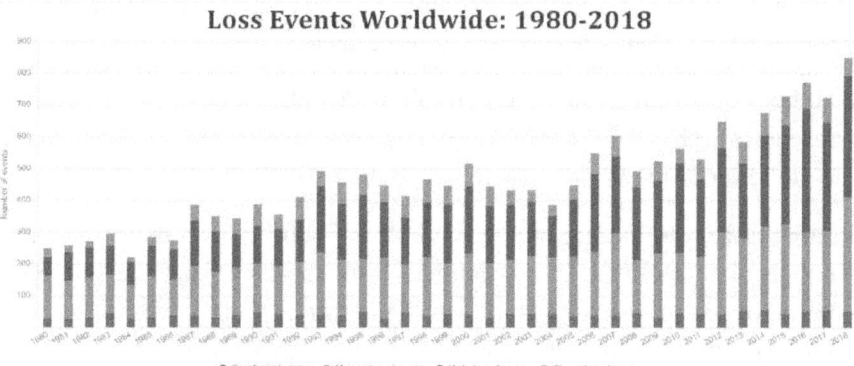

Source: MunichRe - NatCatService

The above graph comes not from a prophecy website, but from a major information service that provides analysis of natural disasters for insurance companies. The trend in the above graph is clear.

One of the typical ways non-believers try to explain away this trend is by saying the world's population has increased, so, according to them, we're just seeing more damage and lost lives due to that.

Yet, the *number* of significant natural disasters (not measured in lives lost or damage incurred, but simply the number of events) was approximately 225 in 1980. By 2018, that number had risen to 848. A growth of 277%!

In that same period of time, the global population has only increased from 4.5 billion to 7.63 billon, a mere 70% increase.

Even just comparing recent years reveals something dramatic. Just between 2015 and 2018, the number of natural disasters increased from 750 to 848. That's an increase of 13% in just three years. Global population and new construction growth have *not* increased at anywhere near that rate.

Natural disasters have increased at more than 4 times the rate of the population growth. Not to mention the large majority of the global population increase has occurred within the same large cities, not in new cities located in new geographical areas, so the actual relationship between these two rates of increase is even more drastic.

Another excuse given is that we simply have better reporting today. This is nonsensical. The world has had a 24-hour news cycle with reporters around the globe reporting to us instantly since the early 1990's.

Furthermore, the internet has been a strong source of global information since the late 1990's, yet we can see from the chart that the number of natural disasters has increased 88% just since 2005, while the world population in that same time period has only increased 16.7%.

The Sign of Earthquakes (Specifically)

"And there will be great earthquakes in various places..." (Luke 21:11)

"Quakes are increasing, but scientists aren't sure what it means," reported the L.A. Times in 2014.[49] "U.S. Geological Survey reveals dramatic increase in central U.S. earthquakes in recent years," reports a major news outlet in Kansas.[50]

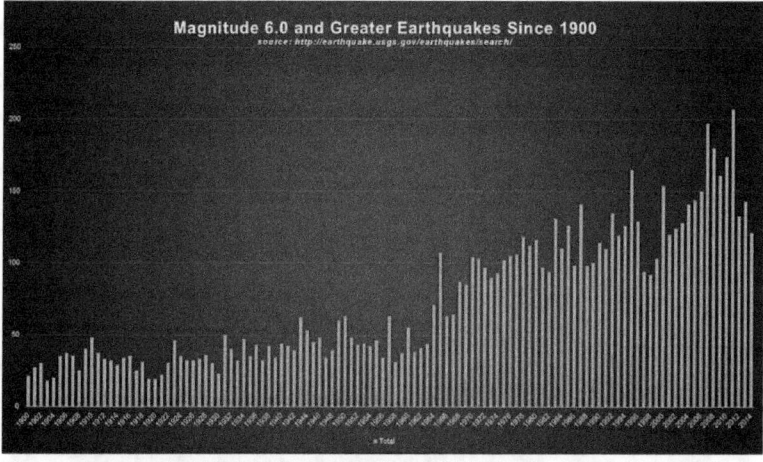

Source: www.psalm11918.org/Resources/Blog/2014/09/is-the-tribulation-near.html

The creator of the above graph (using data from the U.S. Geological Survey) is just one of many who've shown that there has been a significant increase in earthquakes with magnitudes of 6.0 or greater in recent decades. Until the 1960's, the globe hovered around 50 large earthquakes (6.0 or greater) per year. Then, in the mid-1960's, we crossed the 100 quake mark for the first time and stayed there until the late 1970's when around 125 became the new normal. After that, the late 1990's saw us pass the 150 per

---

[49] http://www.latimes.com/local/la-me-la-quakes-20140603-story.html
[50] http://fox4kc.com/2016/09/03/u-s-geological-survey-reveals-dramatic-increase-in-central-u-s-earthquakes-in-recent-years/

year mark, and now in the 2000's, we've not only hit 200 large earthquakes per year, we've passed that mark several times.

Some would argue the leap in the number of recorded quakes is just due to more sensitive or a greater number of sensors being deployed, but that is not supported by data. There have not been 50% more sensors deployed in the last ten years. Furthermore, 6.0 quakes are so significant that we've had sufficiently sensitive sensors to detect them for a long time. In short, these arguments do not hold water. There is a clear increase.

For further evidence, see the following chart (again derived from U.S. Geological Survey data) which totals the amount of total explosive energy released by global earthquakes for each five-year period since the 1980's. (Explosive power is calculated by averaging the estimated equivalent of each quake in terms of tons of TNT for each magnitude level).

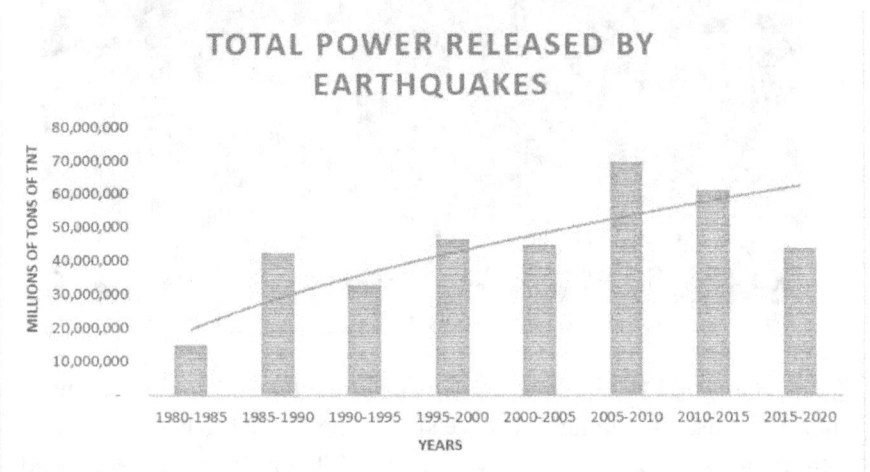

This is truly a sign of change.

A moderate increase in the sensitivity or number of sensors around the world does not account for a registering of almost 400% more explosive energy released between 2005-2010 when compared with 1980-1985.

Especially since we are not considering any quakes less than 5.0 for this study.

The above means that between 1980-1985, earthquakes around the world released the equivalent of 15 million tons of TNT. Yet, the power released both between 2005-2010 and 2010-2015 was in each period well over 60 million tons of TNT. Such a huge difference is comparable to over 11,000 nuclear bombs set off in the earth's crust during a five-year period. It is not believable that we didn't have sensitive enough equipment in the 1980's to detect over ten thousand nuclear bombs.

On an interesting note, the creator of the first graph delves deeper into the data and tries to prove that the number of earthquakes with a magnitude of *7.0* or greater has actually remained flat. They conclude this means nothing has changed…but this is not true.

For one, Jesus warned that first would come the "labor pains." 6.0 quakes are large enough to cause significant damage and some loss of life, but they are not nearly as devastating as a 7.0. It is just like our merciful God to increase the number of quakes at the lower magnitude 6 level *first* in order to get our attention.

Just as a woman beginning labor will experience cramps that are serious, but never as serious as the final contractions at the time of delivery, so should we expect the severity of earthquakes to strengthen over time.

Second, the U.S. Geological survey states that they normally "expect about 16 major earthquakes in any given year" and that the world has only exceeded that average 12 times since 1973.[51] The years this has happened are: 1976, 1990, 1995, 1999, 2007, 2009, 2010, 2011, 2013, 2015, 2016, and 2018.

However, the reader will notice that 92% of those years are in the 1990s or later, and that 50% of them occurred within the past 10 years. All of which seems to say the earth's labor pains have indeed begun. If this is correct, then the more serious quakes are to come.

---

[51] https://www.usgs.gov/faqs/why-are-we-having-so-many-earthquakes-has-naturally-occurring-earthquake-activity-been?qt-news_science_products=0#qt-news_science_products

The Sign of Famine & Pestilences

*"And there will be...**famines and pestilences;** and there will be fearful sights and great signs from heaven."*
(Luke 21:11)

When I first sat down to begin writing this book five years ago, I wrote that this was one of the few signs that seemed to have not yet been fulfilled. Of course, we'd had localized famines like what happened in Africa in the 1980s and minor outbreaks of disease but nothing big enough to merit a mention by Jesus.

One could consider the AIDS epidemic one of the first global pestilences of modern times, and it's noteworthy that there have been several severe Ebola outbreaks in Africa recently.

Then came the year 2020 and Coronavirus. I don't have to tell you about Coronavirus. You've lived it. For the first time in global history, the entire world locked itself down, closing schools and businesses, canceling sports, and limiting gatherings in order to slow the spread.

I'd say we *definitely* have a true global pestilence on our hands that more than qualifies for a mention in prophecy. The world's never been impacted this way by a disease before (whether or not the lockdowns were actually the right solution or not is irrelevant, its impact was unquestionably profound on every nation).

And some health experts like Dr. Fauci of the National Institute of Allergy and Infectious Diseases (NIAID) have been predicting more waves of Coronavirus and new strains of a mutated Swine Flu.

Pestilences? Check.

So, what about famines? As of this writing, the UN World Food Relief is warning that the Coronavirus lockdowns are going to provoke a global famine "of biblical proportions."[52] (I love how people use the phrase of "biblical proportions" to mean really big and bad.)

On top of this, agriculturalists have been warning that massive swarms of locusts are developing in Africa and Asia.[53] Already many of these swarms have descended on Kenya, Ethiopia, and Somalia.[54] "Luck" has favored the farmers so far. They have not been successful in reducing the swarms with pesticides, but the winds have kept them away from croplands. As soon as winds change in the wrong direction, however, massive famine is expected.

For whichever reason, or both, it seems that large famines are very possible in the near future.

---

[52] https://www.theguardian.com/global-development/2020/apr/21/coronavirus-pandemic-will-cause-famine-of-biblical-proportions
[53] https://news.yahoo.com/massive-locust-swarm-africa-middle-144211394.html
[54] https://www.washingtonpost.com/graphics/world/2020/05/05/locusts-africa-swarms-kenya-ethiopia/

The Sign of Martyrdom

"... Then shall they deliver you up to be afflicted and shall kill you: and ye shall be hated of all nations for my name's sake. And then shall many be offended, and shall betray one another, and shall hate one another."
(Matthew 24:9-10)

Throughout history, Christians have been martyred for their faith – but the question is: Are Christian martyrdoms increasing?

From the massacres of Christians in South Sudan[55] and Nigeria[56], to church attacks in Pakistan[57], Indonesia[58], Egypt[59] and France[60], to the graphic images of the Islamic State beheading Christians on the beach, *there is no denying that the murder of Christians globally has suddenly increased in recent years.*

(I urge the reader to visit the links below to read about brothers and sisters in Christ who are suffering and need our help.)

According to a report commissioned by the British government, religious persecution is reaching epidemic proportions with the most persecuted group by far being Christians. UK Foreign Secretary Jeremy Hunt says Christian persecution is at "near genocide levels."[61]

Yet, the Book of Revelation says that the martyrdom of God's people begins on a mass scale with the breaking of the fifth seal, which comes after

---

[55] http://www.christianpost.com/news/south-sudan-untold-number-christians-massacred-thousands-taking-refuge-churches-ceasefire-begins-166397/
[56] http://www.christianpost.com/news/radical-islamist-herdsmen-kill-500-nigerian-christians-over-month-villagers-afraid-to-bury-their-dead-159303/
[57] http://edition.cnn.com/2016/03/27/asia/pakistan-lahore-deadly-blast/
[58] https://www.theguardian.com/world/2016/aug/29/man-armed-with-suicide-bomb-and-axe-attacks-church-in-indonesia
[59] https://www.opendoorsusa.org/take-action/pray/more-easter-attacks-church-in-egypt-burned-to-the-ground-in-minutes/
[60] http://www.reuters.com/article/us-france-hostages-idUSKCN1060VA
[61] https://www.bbc.com/news/uk-48146305

other large events. Unfortunately, this means that we haven't really seen anything yet like the persecution that is coming our way in the future.

Regardless, it can be said this sign is beginning to come true.

The Sign of the Completion of the Great Commission

> *"... And this Gospel of the Kingdom shall be preached in all the world for a witness unto all nations; and then shall the end come." (Matthew 24:14)*

In 1999, Wycliffe Bible Translators announced a project called Vision 2025. The purpose of the project was to rapidly accelerate the translation of the Bible into every language in the world so that every person on earth could have access to it. The goal of the project is to see a Bible translation project begun for every language group by the year 2025.

As it stands, the Bible holds the record (by a *large* margin) for the most-translated book, as well as the widest-published book in the history of the world. With over *5 billion* copies already sold, and an additional 100 million sold every year, the Bible is already considered to be the best-selling book of all time.[62]

In fact, while there are still a large number of languages without a complete Bible, Wycliffe and others estimate that the number of people groups that have not yet seen a Bible translation project started is now only around 180 million people out of 7 billion.[63]

This number has dropped significantly from the launch of the project in 1999. At the rate Wycliffe is going, it is very probable that they will fully meet their goal by 2025.[64]

And wherever a Bible project has begun, you have missionaries on site, living with the people, learning their language, and *sharing the Gospel*. Therefore, while it could be argued that the Gospel has already been preached in "all the world" – and it has – it appears that within the next

---

[62] https://www.guinnessworldrecords.com/world-records/best-selling-book-of-non-fiction
[63] http://www.wycliffe.net/statistics
[64] https://www.missionfrontiers.org/pdfs/28-4-cresson.pdf

decade, the Gospel will have been preached to every tribe, tongue, and nation...*literally.*

The Sign of the Completion of the Great Commission cannot be said to have ever been true before. This is clearly something new ... and it is happening now.

Revisiting the words of Jesus, he said that once the Gospel was preached to every nation, *then* "the end would come."

What Can We Conclude?

There are at most 19 signs of the end times that must be true at the same time to know we have reached the last days. Of those, all 19 are now true. There are at least 3 more that we would expect to start seeing by now, and we are indeed seeing those begin.

We should also expect many of these signs to only grow more intense over time.

So, all the signs God has given us to look for are being fulfilled, and we have nothing else we are supposed to look for other than these signs. Therefore, it is very reasonable for a believer of Scripture to conclude that we are indeed entering a special time of prophetic fulfillment.

The Seals

The 1ˢᵗ Seal

MANY CHRISTIANS TODAY believe they will be raptured (taken up from the earth supernaturally) to meet Christ in the clouds *before* the antichrist is revealed. This belief is called the Pre-Tribulation Rapture.

The word Tribulation is a Christian term, related to the word "trouble," referring to seven specific years in the future of great persecution for followers of Christ. This period is predicted in Revelation and other prophecy sections of Scripture. To believe in a Pre-Tribulation Rapture means you believe God is going to protect all current believers from the coming trouble.

However, because Revelation mentions believers being martyred after the Tribulation begins, it is said these are people who must come to believe in Christ after, or even because of, the Rapture.

While the Rapture is indeed a correct biblical belief, the specific Pre-Tribulation timing of the Rapture is really *not* supported by the Bible.

Christians who believe in a *Pre*-Tribulation Rapture are likely to be caught very much by surprise and unprepared. While the Rapture event is very real (Scripture does teach that we will be caught up to meet Christ in the air), this commonly understood timing is wrong.

Pre-Tribulation teachers know their position is not clearly and explicitly supported by the text of Revelation, as the Apostle John makes no reference to it happening before the Tribulation in his vision.

So, they use an "argument of silence" to make their case. Proponents say that the word "church" appears many times before Chapter 4 of Revelation, but then does not reappear until Chapter 22, which is after the Second Coming of Christ.

They argue that because the word "church" is not used in the intervening chapters, this means the church must be physically absent from the world during that time. (Note: an argument from silence is a weak argument).

However, by admitting that Chapters 4 and 22 represent specific chronological moments in the timeline of events, they are admitting that the Book of Revelation is to be interpreted chronologically!

With that point admitted by all, then why are we ignoring Chapter 14 when it does clearly describe a Rapture-like event?

Also, the Bible teaches that *all* believers form the eternal Church, the Body of Christ. That means that as soon as there are new believers on earth after the Rapture, the Church would be considered present again. Therefore, their argument is self-defeating.

The Rapture Will *Not* Occur *Before* the Tribulation

In Revelation 14, it says:

> *"Then I looked, and behold, a white cloud, and **on the cloud sat One like the Son of Man**, having **on His head a golden crown**, and in His hand a sharp sickle. And another angel came out of the temple, crying with a loud voice to Him who sat on the cloud, "Thrust in Your sickle and reap, for the time has come for You to reap, for the harvest of the earth is ripe." **So, He who sat on the cloud thrust in His sickle on the earth, and the earth was reaped."** (Revelation 14:14-16)*

All the other beings described in Revelation 14 are called angels. Only here does it say "One like the Son of Man" – a title belonging to Christ.

Also, no one in Heaven has a crown but Jesus. Therefore, Revelation 14 can be nothing but a clear image of Jesus on a cloud harvesting His followers from the earth.

Especially since the verses following this passage describe a second and distinct harvest performed by a lesser angel immediately after the first. That angel throws every single person he harvests into the "winepress of the wrath of God." Since this second "harvest" is all about wrath, the previous harvest done by the Son of Man has to be for blessing or salvation.

There can be no doubt the first harvest is describing the Rapture – and it occurs in Chapter 14, *after* the appearance of the antichrist in Chapter 6. In other words, the Rapture happens *after* the arrival of the antichrist.

Long after.

Truly, the only reason the Pre-Tribulation Rapture belief took root was from a desire by believers to avoid the Great Persecution.

Yet, the blood of Jesus saves us from the Wrath of God, but not man. God never promises to save believers from the wrath of men or the enemy. Actually, by accepting the covering of Jesus' blood, we have agreed to pick up our personal cross and be subjected to the same persecution our King suffered.

In the chronology of Revelation, all the troubles of the early parts of the Tribulation are attributable to the wrath of men and the enemy. The Wrath of God does not begin until the bowl judgments, which are in Chapter 15...*curiously the chapter immediately after Chapter 14.*

The Arrival of the Antichrist

> *"Now I saw when the Lamb opened one of the seals; and I heard one of the four living creatures saying with a voice like thunder, "Come and see." And I looked, and behold, a white horse. He who sat on it had a bow; and a crown was given to him,* **and he went out conquering and to conquer."** *(Revelation 6:1-2)*

> *"... Let no man deceive you by any means: for that day shall not come, except...that man of sin be revealed, the son of perdition." (2 Thessalonians 2:3)*

We left our study of Revelation in Chapter 5 where we saw the Lamb of God taking possession of the double-sided scroll. All of Heaven has declared only He is worthy to take it, and we believe the scroll is the real estate deed to the earth.

The scroll is sealed with 7 seals. A wax seal was an ancient method of keeping a document confidential and tamper-proof before the intended recipient received it.

In Chapter 6, prophetic end time events finally begin to unfurl. In order to claim what is rightfully His (the earth and its people), the Lamb of God begins breaking each of the seals one by one so he can unroll the document.

When He breaks the 1st Seal, a rider on a white horse rides forth. This author has never read a commentary that did not interpret the white horse and rider as a symbol for the arrival of the antichrist. Surely there are some out there, but this is a commonly held understanding, so we don't need to prove it.

So, Who Is the Antichrist?

We're going to take a good stab at answering that question for you using all of the other biblical prophecies about him and matching those up with current events. Yet, first we must pose a question:

What kind of antichrist are *you* expecting?

Ask most Evangelical Americans what they know about the antichrist, and they'll tell you he's going to be a man of peace (usually from Rome), a charismatic leader the whole world loves who is ushered into office through great popularity. They believe he's going to sign a seven-year peace treaty with Israel, which allows Israel to rebuild God's Temple, but that in the middle of the seven-year period, he will show his true colors and begin attacking God's people everywhere.

Essentially, it's believed he will destroy through deception, through peace treaties that he does not intend to keep.

Yet, this understanding is based on several misconceptions about the antichrist that have been taught over decades as fact.

If we're looking for the wrong things, we might not recognize him in time, and the potential danger of not recognizing the antichrist in time should be obvious …

There are many commonly held expectations by American Christians that do *not* have Biblical support. You may be surprised to discover that a close reading of Scripture reveals:

- The antichrist's arrival does *not* launch the seven-year Tribulation.
- The antichrist will *not* be a man of peace.
- The antichrist will *not* be European.
- The antichrist might *not* sign a treaty with *Israel*

Before we get into the meat of our study, we first need to examine those four misconceptions better. Our prayer is that believers everywhere will take a fresh look at Scripture after reading this and open their eyes to new possibilities.

The Arrival of the Antichrist Does *Not* Launch the Seven-Year Tribulation

Revelation 6:2 says the antichrist (the rider on the white horse) is given power when the Lamb breaks the 1st seal. Many have taught that this moment initiates the long foretold seven-year Tribulation.

Yet, a careful examination of Revelation clarifies that the seven-year Tribulation period begins in Revelation 11 with the arrival of God's two Witnesses, *not* when the antichrist shows up in Revelation 6 at the breaking of the 1st seal.

Daniel was a prophet of Israel who lived in the 5th century BC. God worked through him in powerful ways during the time Judah was still in captivity in Babylon and then Persia. The book that bears his name in the Bible is a record of some of what God did and spoke through him. In it are recorded numerous prophecies about future events, some of which have since come true, others are still to come.

Daniel prophesied several times about the evil one to come at the end of days. Daniel 9:27 says the antichrist will *at some point* enter into a seven-year treaty with "many." It does *not* say whether Israel is a party to this treaty. It could be, it could not be. Time will tell. It also does not say that the execution of this treaty marks the beginning of the antichrist's coming into power.

Logically, the antichrist would have to already be in a significant position of power to effect a treaty with "many," and it takes time to conquer, and even more time to solidify power.

Daniel 9:27 also says that halfway through the seven-year treaty period, the antichrist will enter the Temple (reconstructed in Jerusalem) and put an end to the sacrifices.

Revelation 11 says that Two Witnesses (many believe they are Moses & Elijah returned, but more on this later ...) testify about God and the coming judgment in Jerusalem for *three and a half years*, and that any who try to kill them then are destroyed by fire coming from their mouths.

After those first three and a half years, the antichrist finally succeeds in killing them. Then, he enters the Temple, stops the Jewish sacrifices, and persecutes Israel and the Church for another *three and a half years*.

$$3.5 \text{ years} + 3.5 \text{ years} = 7 \text{ years}$$

Therefore, the entire seven-year Tribulation will be taken up by the years allocated to the two Witnesses followed by the persecution of Israel.

Of course, when we read Revelation chronologically, this makes perfect sense for Revelation 11 (two Witnesses) comes long after Chapter 6 and many other destructive events described in the intermediate chapters.

So, the antichrist will have to begin his conquest *("conquering and to conquer")* at least several years before the treaty could be negotiated, and the negotiations would presumably also take months (at least).

Based on the layout of Revelation, all seven seals would be broken and six of the seven trumpets would sound before this treaty of prophesy and the appearance of the two Witnesses. (We'll get to the other seals and the trumpets soon – for now don't worry about it.)

What is now clear is that the 1st seal of the Lamb must be broken years before the signing of the treaty — *and there is no specific statement limiting that time interval.*

Our expectation should be that the antichrist will begin his military conquest at least three to five years before the treaty would be signed.

Still, because the Bible does not define the time interval, he could even begin as early as twenty to thirty years prior. (However, any longer than that and we'd have to assume he'd have grown too old to continue.)

The Antichrist Will *Not* Be a Man of Peace

"Through complacency, he shall destroy many" (Daniel 8:25)

Believe it or not, the *entire* idea that the antichrist will begin as a man of peace is based on a single verse, Daniel 8:25 (and a bad translation of it to boot), combined with a weak inference from Revelation 6:2.

The King James is one of the few English translations where Daniel 8:25 reads *"through peace, he shall destroy many."* That translation has inspired countless scholars to speculate that the antichrist will conquer through deceptive peace treaties, primarily because another part of the verse describes how the antichrist will cause *"deceit to prosper."*

However, the word translated "peace" in the King James is not the Hebrew *shalom,* but instead *shalvah.*

Shalvah does not mean peace but "to be at ease from prosperity" or "at ease from a sense of security." Thus, the best translation of Daniel 8:25 is *"through complacency, he shall destroy many,"* which is a perfect description of how groups like the Islamic State have conquered while the West sits complacent.

There are literally *no* other verses to support the idea that the antichrist will be a man of peace. In contrast, Revelation 6:2 says he goes out *"conquering and to conquer."* Conquering is violent. This is not a description of one who comes into power through an election.

The only other support for the antichrist being a man of peace is that very same verse where it says in Revelation 6:2 the antichrist has a bow. Some argue that because a bow is described, but not arrows, he must be peaceful.

Unfortunately, arguing from silence (no mention of arrows) is again a very weak argument, and it certainly is in this case. Mentioning the bow does not require a mention of arrows, nor does it require a mention of a quiver, or archery gloves, etc.

It is much more likely the bow is specifically mentioned to make sure this figure is not confused with the person of Jesus Christ who comes at the end of Revelation on a white horse as well, but He with a sword, that sword being the Word of God.

The significance of the bow could be literal, indicating the antichrist will possess missile systems (possibly nuclear ones). It could also be a comment on the fact that historically knights and other warriors regarded the bow as a coward's weapon, meaning the antichrist is without honor in how he does battle.

Regardless, he will go out "conquering and to conquer." We should be expecting a man of violence, not a man of peace. Here are some of the other titles given the antichrist in Scripture:

- The Bloody and Deceitful Man (Ps. 5:6)
- The Wicked One (Ps. 10:2-4)
- The Enemy (Ps 10:18)
- The Adversary (Ps. 74:8-10)
- The Violent One (Ps. 140:1)
- The Profane Wicked Prince (Ezek. 21:25-27)
- The Vile Person (Dan. 11:21)

- The Man of Sin (2 Thess. 2:3)
- The Son of Perdition (2 Thess. 2:3)
- The Lawless One (2 Thess. 2:8)
- The Beast (Rev. 11:7)
- The Abomination of Desolation (Matt. 24:15)
- The Desolator (Dan 9:27)

None of these titles indicate he will be charismatic or beloved by anyone. It is dangerous for so many believers to be looking for the wrong kind of man.

The Antichrist Will *Not* Be "Roman" or European

It is commonly believed by many Christians that the antichrist will be "Roman" and rule over a revived Roman Empire in Europe.

This has been repeated over and over by numerous books and teachers. Yet, just as with the idea the antichrist would be a man of peace, support from the Bible for this concept is very limited. In fact, the *only* biblical support for him being a European is a *single* verse: Daniel 9:26. It reads:

*"...and the **people** of the prince who is to come shall destroy the city and the sanctuary."*

No one doubts the "prince who is to come" is the antichrist, and everyone knows that the Romans are the ones who destroyed the Temple of God in 70 AD. Thus, the idea that the antichrist would be Roman is a natural interpretation here for Bible students.

However, while the soldiers who destroyed the Temple were technically part of the Roman army, it is known from historical documents that, in terms of nationality and race, *none of those soldiers were actually Roman.* The soldiers who destroyed Jerusalem and the Temple belonged to the Legion *X Fretensis*[65], along with three other legions. This legion was based

---

[65] https://en.wikipedia.org/wiki/Legio_X_Fretensis

in the City of Antioch (now within the borders of Turkey, and its men had been recruited by Rome from what is today Turkey and Syria. The other legions played lesser roles, but similarly their recruits were from the areas of modern-day Turkey and Syria. In fact, modern scholars have determined that the only members of that army two thousand years ago who likely had actual Roman blood coursing through their veins were the officers.[66]

Titus, the Roman general who led siege did everything in his power that day to *not* destroy the Temple, but the Turk and Syrian soldiers hated the Jewish people so much that they blatantly disobeyed his and the orders of other Roman officers. The Temple was actually burned and destroyed in contradiction to Roman orders.[67]

It is telling that the verse does not say "the kingdom of the prince who is to come" but "the *people* of the prince who is to come." This is the Hebrew word *'am* (עַם), which corresponds to the Greek *ethnos, i.e. "ethnicity."* That word choice lends itself to an interpretation that the antichrist will hail from the lands of ancient Assyria.

To confirm this, the prophets Isaiah and Micah both called the antichrist "the Assyrian" (Isaiah 10:24-25[68] and Micah 5:3-6). The ancient kingdom of Assyria occupied the lands which are today Turkey, Syria, and Iraq – the same regions that birthed the soldiers who destroyed God's Temple in 70 AD.

Curiously, the shape of the lands recently occupied by the Islamic State resembled the same territory controlled by ancient Assyria.

---

[66] Soldiers, Cities, and Civilians in Roman Syria (University of Michigan Press, 2000) Nigel Pollard, Ph.D.,
[67] https://revelation-now.org/wp-content/uploads/The-People-of-Baal-Destroyed-the-Temple-in-70-AD.pdf
[68] Note: The NIV does not appear to be the best translation of these verses.

Does the Antichrist Sign a Treaty with *Israel*?

It's possible, but this author doesn't believe so. The teaching that the antichrist signs a 7-year treaty *with Israel* comes from Daniel 9:27:

*"Then he shall confirm a covenant with **many** for one week ..."*

The "he" in that verse is the antichrist, and the "covenant" is a treaty or an accord between nations. The phrase "one week" means one week *of years*, or seven years.

We notice, though, that it does *not* say he makes a covenant with Israel, but with "many." The many *could* include Israel, but most likely not, especially when one considers the hatred Muslim nations have toward Israel.

In discussions about prophecy, many teachers forget about or are unaware of the 83rd Psalm, but that passage is key for a better understanding of the whole picture of prophecy. Psalm 83 is a prophetic psalm describing a war against Israel which the open-minded reader will realize has not happened yet.

It describes a coalition of *ten* "peoples" who form a confederacy among themselves solely for the purpose of destroying Israel forever.

Ten is a very significant number in prophecy and should jump out at anyone familiar at all with either the Books of Daniel or Revelation.

From those books, it has long been known that the antichrist's empire, otherwise known as "the beast," would consist of ten nations. In both Daniel and Revelation, the beast has ten "horns" which represent ten kings of ten unnamed peoples (at least not named in those passages).

Yet, there is another place in the Bible where specifically ten peoples are *named* in reference to such a confederation against Israel: Psalm 83.

The ten peoples listed there correspond to the Muslim nations surrounding Israel today. These are the very same nations who have "last days" judgments pronounced against them in the books of Isaiah, Jeremiah, Ezekiel, and others. (This is amazing consistency from different prophets who lived hundreds of years apart from each other and were predicting events thousands of years in the future.)

> *"For they have consulted together with one consent;*
> *They form a confederacy against You ..." (Psalm 83:5)*

Of course, any confederacy requires a treaty. One cannot have a formal alliance of nations toward any end without some kind of formalized written agreement between them, which is typically called a treaty.

> *"Assyria also has joined with them" (Psalm 83:8)*

That verse comes at the end of the list, after nine other peoples who band together against Israel. In Psalm 83:8, the word "with" is better translated as "among," "before," or "together." So, the best translation is probably "And Assyria has joined them together."

Thus, Psalm 83 implies that Assyria leads this confederacy — again, a description of Assyria in the lead to destroy Israel.

Since all of Israel's enemies, who are slated by God for judgment in the Old Testament, are Muslim nations today, it is worthwhile to examine Islam as a religion and understand why.

If Islam is a "peaceful" religion, and if Islam is really a "sister" belief system with Christianity, then why do Muslims persecute Jews and Christians so virulently around the world?

The Nature of Islam

Mohammed said that the way the Koran came to him was that one day, he was in a cave, and a dark angel attacked him and began to suffocate and strangle him. The dark angel repeated the action several times, demanding that Mohammed recite the words of the Koran. Finally, when Mohammed could take no more, he finally began to recite the Koran.[69]

---

[69] http://www.answering-islam.org/Authors/JR/Future/ch11_the_dark_nature.htm

After this, he was tormented and so convinced that he was demon-possessed that he became suicidal. Over time, he continued to recite more pieces of the Koran, but each time, before he began, he would go into an epileptic fit (another sign of demon possession).

The spirit of Islam can only be described as violent and oppressive. An objective reading of the Koran confirms this. The method of Islam is to spread itself through war and bloodshed. This is the only way it has spread throughout history.

First, let's get something clear. "Muslim" is not a race. A Muslim is a person who chooses to identify themselves with the religion of Islam, which relates to thinking, belief, and philosophy and is a choice, but has nothing to do with race, national origin, or genetics.

Therefore, since to be Muslim is to ally oneself with a specific form of thinking, and it is legitimate to oppose certain lines of thinking, then it is also legitimate to be "anti-Muslim," meaning against the thinking or religion, but not the individual as a person. We love all people and value them, but we can be against how they think, their beliefs, and/or practices.

In fact, to consider "Muslim" a race, is to marginalize the hundreds of thousands of Middle Eastern Christians, Jews, Bahai, and other faiths. Arab is a race, not Muslim. We love the Arabian people of all faiths, but Islamic beliefs and practices are problematic.

When Muslims are lukewarm in their faith, not committed or passionate, they are peaceful and hospitable. Honestly, most "Muslims" are like that today. The large majority of citizens of Muslim nations only call themselves Muslim because they happened to be born into a Muslim country, but they aren't truly dedicated to Muslim theology. They might or might not attend mosque regularly. They don't do the prayers faithfully, or travel to Mecca or read the Koran.

If you travel to most Muslim countries, you will find a friendly and hospitable people in so many places. I have personally participated in mission trips to Muslim peoples across the world and fell in love with the warm people who welcomed me into their homes. And this truly was the case in most homes.

However, there was always a small part of the people (maybe around 10%?) who stared at us through narrowed, hostile eyes as we walked down the street, hatred etched in every line of their face. Those are the radicals. When Muslims fully dedicate themselves to their faith and become committed followers of Mohammad and the Koran, that is when the anger and violence start.

This is the opposite of Christianity. Christ called His followers to expand His Kingdom through self-sacrifice and humility, through love and turning the other cheek. Throughout history, Christianity has only spread successfully through these means.

The Crusades failed because the church has never successfully expanded Christianity through force. Historically, when force is tried by Christians, it fails. Only through self-sacrifice and love does the Kingdom grow.

Yet, just like in Muslim countries, Christian countries are plagued by people who call themselves Christian but don't really follow Jesus. Ashley Madison, a website that works to help people cheat on their spouses, recently announced their membership is spiking in many American cities.

Most Americans today call themselves Christian, but very few follow Jesus well. They aren't attending church regularly or reading the Bible. They aren't giving of themselves sacrificially, neither financially nor by donating time in service. Faith, for most Americans, has become a side thing, a series of pet beliefs they may or may not hold depending on how much time they've dedicated to actually thinking about them, but they're typically not committed enough to allow God to shape them, transform them, or even require any change to their behavior.

When we find a Christian believer who is passionate about their faith, we expect them to be kind, loving and honorable. If not, we immediately view them as a hypocrite.

Not the same for a Muslim, if we are honest. We would expect a dedicated Muslim to be possibly considering *jihad*. (Especially since *jihad* is an integral part of Islamic belief and practice.)

Honest people understand there is a strong difference between the two faiths. Only people with an agenda to not acknowledge Christianity as superior insist all religions are the same.

Did you know that Islam also has many end time prophecies? Muslims have a messianic figure they call the *mahdi*.

In *Islamic* prophecy, the *mahdi* does the exact same things the antichrist does in the Bible - even to the point Muslims say the *mahdi* will meet for a final battle in the valley of Armageddon against a figure from Jerusalem claiming to be Jesus. (Of course, Christians believe that figure will be the real Jesus.)

Jesus said that in the last days there would be many who killed Christians because they thought they were doing a service to God.

Revelation is clear in its description of a world where the difference between being marked by God for salvation and for damnation is whether or not one *worships* the beast. Repeat: the word "worship" is used.

Therefore, the antichrist *will* have a religion. He cannot be an atheistic, communist dictator and still fulfill the sense of that prophecy. Understanding this, some have speculated the antichrist would establish a novel, global "New Age" religion with himself as the focus of worship. An organized religion that does not yet exist.

This seems like grasping. Frankly, they only pursue this line of thought because of a misguided attempt to force prophecy into a European-centric interpretation. Yet, this is fallacy because the Bible is always Middle East-centric.

And in the Middle East, there's already an existing religion that hates Israel, demonstrates the spirit of antichrist in that it stands against everything Jesus ever commanded or taught, and was clearly inspired by demons.

If Islam was inspired by demons who possessed Mohammad, if it inspires violence and hatred of God's people (Jews and Christians), and if it stands against the teachings of Jesus, then it is, frankly, the religion of the devil.

And if Islam is the religion of the devil, then what other religion would the antichrist espouse?

Understanding this, the only thing we're waiting for is an Islamic Caliphate (Islamic Superpower) to arise ... *and that is now becoming a reality.*

The Mahdi is the Antichrist

The Muslim messiah is called the *mahdi*. Muslims have a lot of end-time prophecies about this figure, all of which seem to mirror the prophecies in the Bible about the antichrist.

Here are some of the correlations:

THE BIBLE	ISLAM
The antichrist will rule many nations, especially the *enemies* of Israel.	The mahdi is supposed to unite the Muslim world into an Islamic Caliphate.
The antichrist enters into a seven-year treaty with "many."	The mahdi *also* rules a coalition of nations for seven years.
The antichrist will have *a false prophet* who is able to call down fire from heaven and tells everyone to worship the antichrist.	The mahdi has a right-hand man, a *prophet* who can call down fire from heaven and tells everyone to submit to the mahdi. Muslims say this prophet will claim to be Jesus returned to earth, which from a Christian perspective would make him a false prophet.
Jesus said, "Therefore if they say to you, 'Look, He is in the desert!' do not go out; or 'Look, He is in the inner rooms!' do not believe it."	Muslims say their "Jesus" (false prophet) will appear at a mosque in Damascus (Damascus is in the desert).

The antichrist will stop the sacrifices in the Temple and put his image there.	The mahdi will set up his throne in Jerusalem on the Temple Mount.
The Bible is clear that Jesus will first set foot on the Mount of Olives outside Jerusalem when He returns. After this, Jesus will destroy the antichrist in the valley of Megiddo (Armageddon).	Islam says the mahdi fights a final battle in the valley of Megiddo against a man from Jerusalem claiming to be Jesus who leads an army of Jews. (This *is* the real Jesus, but Muslims will deny it.)

Based on these correlations, it is easy to see that Christianity and Islam have exact polar opposite prophecies regarding the end times. Islam calls what is good, bad, and what is bad, good — as usual.

What Are We Waiting On?

Honestly? *Nothing.*

Meaning, there are *zero* major prophetic events that must occur before the Lamb of God breaks the first seal.

The Rapture happens long *after* the appearance of the two witnesses. The antichrist will already be in place when the seven-year treaty is signed, regardless of who he signs it with.

The only thing we are waiting for is the appearance of the antichrist on the world scene.

When the lawless one begins to conquer, we'll know the Lamb has broken the first seal and the events of Revelation have begun to unfold.

We know the biblical signs pointing to the arrival of the end times are all coming true simultaneously, a strong indicator we are now in the last days.

Therefore, the question simply becomes: Do we see any good candidates for the antichrist on the world scene right now?

Almost ready to tackle that subject, but first we must analyze one more major event and its impact on the prophetic timeline.

THE BIRTH OF THE ISLAMIC STATE

BEGINNING WITH 9/11, alongside Al Qaeda, there began to grow a cancerous tumor in the Middle East. It grew at a slow but steady pace for a decade or so, but then separated and became its very own beast. This beast called itself the Islamic State of Iraq.

Through the Arab Spring, the beast found itself fed with weapons and money by siphoning off resources meant for other groups, and in June of 2014, Abu Bakr al Baghdadi, the leader of this entity, declared them to be a worldwide caliphate. From that point forward they would shorten their name to be just the Islamic State.

The Islamic State grew large enough to control much of the territory of Syria and Iraq as well as areas in Libya, Yemen, Nigeria, Niger, Chad and Cameroon, Uzbekistan, and elsewhere.[70] Not just a terrorist organization, it had an internal police force, issued birth certificates, and even fishing licenses.

In 2017, the Trump administration got very serious about taking the fight to the Islamic State, and at the time of this publishing, ISIS has been pushed back to a tiny fraction of its original territory in Syria and Iraq, though they remain with a presence in many other countries. In spite of this, we believe understanding the why and how of the Islamic State is key to understanding future prophetic events.

How the Islamic State Conquered

The Islamic State demonstrated serious prowess in not just conducting terrorist attacks, but in conquering territory and holding it. They did so

---

[70] https://en.wikipedia.org/wiki/ISIL_territorial_claims

seemingly against all odds. Neither the Iraqi nor the Syrian nor the Yemeni governments were able to stop them.

In fact, because of the failure of these national governments to put a halt to their progress, the international community was forced to get involved. Yet, the Islamic State somehow continued to resist and even grow in the face of bombings and assaults from the United States and Russia for many years. At times, it almost seemed like there was a kind of supernatural force behind them, propelling them forward.

There is no doubt that the Islamic State is evil, but whatever else they may be, they are extremely methodical and organized.[71] And that is the worst combo you can have.

Historically, whenever evil finds a way to marry itself to a sophisticated organization, terrible things happen. Just think Nazi Germany.

The Islamic State takes territory through a step-by-step process. When they initially decide to take a territory, they first send individual agents to infiltrate and gather intelligence. These agents then begin to recruit local leaders for support, even buying their support with money.

Next, with a complicit support base in place, they begin sporadic terrorist activities in the region to kill or instill fear in any local leadership who remains in opposition to them. This is phase two.

Phase three is the beginning of *dawa,* i.e. public relations, the winning of hearts and minds of the general populace. They distribute propaganda, give away their black flags, and even hold competitions for young people that include eating contests, Koran memorization, and even tugs of war.[72]

Once they have built this base of public support, they initiate phase four, called *hisba*. *Hisba* is the beginning of their religious police. In this phase, they begin enforcing their brand of "morality" with public burning of alcohol, cigarettes, and other contraband. They monitor whether people are

---

[71] http://www.washingtoninstitute.org/uploads/Documents/pubs/ResearchNote29-Zelin.pdf
[72] http://www.washingtoninstitute.org/uploads/Documents/pubs/ResearchNote29-Zelin.pdf

praying on time, whether shop owners are closing for prayer time, etc. In this stage, they also begin providing consumer protection services where products are inspected for quality and expiration dates.

It could be said that stages one and two are about first recruiting leaders and then eliminating the stubborn ones who remain opposed, while stages three and four are about doing the same things, but with the general public.

The last stage is one of complete governance. By the time they reach this phase, the territory is fully under their control *with the support of the local people*. It is for this reason that national governments have no ability to root them out – removing them is impossible when the local people's support is with them and against the government.

It is also for this reason that when God judges the Islamic State, He will be absolutely just to rain down judgment on the entire people and not just the leaders.

How Evil Is the Islamic State?

The atrocities committed by the Islamic State match the worst of modern history. We've watched them slit throats and behead Christians on the beach. We've watched as they've burned men alive in cages, thrown others off the roofs of buildings, and machine-gunned children in the street.

Until now, Nazi Germany was held up as the universal epitome of evil incarnate – but even the Nazis had some *public* restraint. We do *not* wish to minimize the terrible sins of the Nazis in the least, but their evil was colder, more systematic. There is the impression they felt the need to somewhat conceal their massacres behind the walls of concentration camps.

The very existence of concentration camps reveals the Nazis didn't feel free to operate completely in the open. They made an effort to hide their evil.

The Islamic State on the other hand goes beyond even the Nazis, which until now didn't seem possible. It has zero restraint on its evil and it rips its destructive claws into everyone it encounters without distinction. School children are encouraged to publicly play soccer with the heads of their victims in order to desensitize them to violence. They send boys as young as six years old to military training camps, and we can only imagine what happens to them there.

Women and young girls, be they Yazidi, Shiite, or just Sunnis who don't surrender fast enough, are kidnapped and made into sex slaves. If they refuse, the girls themselves are murdered, or in some cases, their family members are slaughtered one by one before their eyes until they submit to sexual advances.

The Islamic State even removes vital organs from its own wounded soldiers while they're still alive and sells them on the black market. There is no limit to their depravity.

Daniel 7:7 says, *"After this I saw in the night visions, and behold, a fourth beast, dreadful and* **terrible,** *exceedingly strong. It had huge iron teeth;* ***it was devouring, breaking in pieces, and trampling the residue with its feet. It was different from all the beasts that were before it..."***

Was the birth of the Islamic State the birth of the long-foretold Beast? Given the description by the prophet Daniel, it certainly seems a good candidate.

(Note: We do not believe the Islamic State *is* the final Beast – we believe it is the precursor.)

Propaganda of the Islamic State

The Islamic State created a propaganda machine that published media pieces equaling the professionalism of Hollywood or New York.[73] From Facebook to Instagram, YouTube and Twitter, they mastered the use of social media to propagate their message and recruit.

---

[73] https://www.theguardian.com/world/2014/oct/07/isis-media-machine-propaganda-war

They created a media channel that produced full-length documentaries and travel shows, and even a glossy online magazine. They produced deceptively alluring media pieces like these, all while simultaneously distributing gruesome images of their massacres and other atrocities.[74] One serves to lure, the other to intimidate.

The worst part is that the general public across the world has inadvertently helped them with distribution, repeatedly sharing the propaganda all over social media.[75] The result was complacent Western cultures shrinking from our duty in disgust and fear while some of their sons and daughters ran off to join the cause that hides its evil behind a veil of lies.

The Economic Strategy of the Islamic State

The Islamic State is very different from your garden-variety terrorist group when it comes to economics. Traditionally, groups like Hamas, Hezbollah, and Al Qaeda have depended on donations from wealthy Arab oil barons and other sympathetic donors.

But this is what made the Islamic State a *state* and not a terrorist organization. They created a true economy that gave it very deep pockets when compared with "terrorist" organizations.

The area selected for conquest by the Islamic State was heavy in oil fields and contained numerous pipelines. Reportedly, at their peak, they were earning at least $1 million per day by selling oil to the black market.[76]

Turkish oil traders (please note the emphasis on *Turkish*) then resold this oil to others, especially the Syrian and Iraqi governments who were unable to resist purchasing oil at low prices in order to minimize the cost of fueling their militaries as they fought the Islamic State.

---

[74] https://www.funker530.com/recent-propaganda-video/ (WARNING: Graphic)
[75] https://theintercept.com/2020/04/19/coronavirus-isis-advice/
[76] http://www.pbs.org/newshour/rundown/islamic-state-group-taking-1-million-per-day-black-market-oil-report-says/

Both of those governments were going further and further into debt to make these purchases. In essence, these Turkish oil traders set up a system where the Syrian and Iraqi governments were funding their enemy in war and going in debt to do so. It is obvious which side would have eventually won if nothing had changed.

The Islamic State also sells museum antiquities on the black market.[77] When they first entered the city of Mosul, which is the modern name for the ancient city of Ninevah, their warriors were issued orders to destroy every image or icon they could find in the town, including the graveyards and the Tomb of Jonah.

However, they were conspicuously ordered to leave the museums full of actual *idols* alone. Those were to be preserved to sell to antiquity smugglers.

This became a pattern. Some estimates say that the Islamic State controlled the equivalent of $12 *billion* in artifacts and other antiquities from sites it has looted.[78] That alone is greater than the annual GDP of 75 countries.

And they tax as well.

"Only the air people breathe is not taxed," said one resident of Syria who found themselves under Islamic State rule.[79] The Islamic State has a very strong bureaucratic system that knows what every one of its citizens has for an income – and taxes them accordingly.

The Washington Post reported that "The Islamic State levies taxes on things including goods sold, utilities such as electricity and water (when they run, that is — in some areas, the electricity is only on for an hour a day), telecommunication companies, cash withdrawals from bank accounts, employee salaries, trucks entering Islamic State-controlled territory at

---

[77] http://www.nytimes.com/2016/01/10/world/europe/iraq-syria-antiquities-islamic-state.html?_r=0
[78] https://www.alaraby.co.uk/english/features/2015/3/14/12-billion-of-iraqi-antiquities-lost-or-destroyed
[79] http://www.theatlantic.com/international/archive/2015/09/isis-territory-taxes-recruitment-syria/403426/

checkpoints, looting archaeological sites and non-Muslim communities in general."[80]

They also collect quite a bit of income from extortion. They threaten businesses and individuals with harm if they don't pay up. They kidnap international aid workers and others and demand ransom from their families. It's estimated they earn as much as $40 million per year this way.

Beyond that, they have seized hundreds of millions of dollars from banks, and even more than that from the sale of confiscated real estate from individuals they've persecuted or executed. They controlled the agricultural and mining markets and earned income from internal sales tax as well as export tariffs.

Lastly, and most tragically, they sell women and children for sex. Sex trafficking is bringing this evil organization an unknown level of financial gain.

Altogether, before the Trump administration's offensive, it seems the Islamic State was generating for itself close to $2 billion per year.[81] Considering that the large majority of its income went to war and military spending, that amount of money is staggering.

To give an idea of the level of military strength this represents, *the Islamic State's military budget was larger than the military spending of the following countries:*

- Syria
- Jordan
- Kenya
- New Zealand
- Cuba
- Lebanon
- Yemen

---

[80] https://www.washingtonpost.com/news/wonk/wp/2015/11/18/how-isis-makes-its-money/
[81] http://www.washingtoninstitute.org/uploads/Documents/testimony/LevittTestimony20141113.pdf

- Hungary
- Slovakia
- Croatia
- Qatar
- Bahrain
- Bulgaria
- And many more

Their income was three times the size of Cuba's military budget, ten times the military spending of most countries in Central and South America, and *twenty* times the military spending of most African nations.

Most shockingly, they almost reached the military spending of Austria, Egypt, Argentina, South Africa, and even Switzerland.[82]

The Mark of the Beast

For centuries, many have speculated about the long prophesied Mark of the Beast and what it will be, look like, etc.

> *"He causes all, both small and great, rich and poor, free and slave, to receive a mark on their right hand or on their foreheads, and that no one may buy or sell except one who has the mark of the name of the beast, or the number of his name. Here is wisdom. Let him who has understanding calculate the number of the beast, for it is the number of a man: His number is 666."*
> (Revelation 13:16-18)

Some have said the mark will be an RFID chip, which is the size of a grain of rice and can be embedded in your hand, powered by your body and tracked by satellite. These chips can be used to carry bank account info and to buy and sell just like a phone or credit card.

---

[82] http://www.globalfirepower.com/defense-spending-budget.asp

However, because the Bible says that taking the mark damns people to hell without redemption, scholars speculate the antichrist will probably require some kind of pledge of worship to him to receive one.

A different interpretation notes that ancient Greeks did not have distinct symbols for numbers from the letters of their alphabet, and thus – like Roman numerals – every Greek letter also corresponds to a specific number to be used in ancient mathematical calculations.

Ancient believers would have been well aware of this fact, and they would also have been well aware that the values of the letters in Jesus' name (in Greek) add up to 888. Since 8 is the biblical number for God (7 is the number of completion, and God is "more than complete"), this was always seen as further proof of the divinity of Jesus. (More on this later.)

Revelation itself instructs us to *calculate* the name of the beast, based on the *number* of its name, so scholars have suggested that the name of the antichrist in Greek would add up to 666. Which would make perfect sense since 6 is the number of man, i.e. less than complete.

However, Revelation also says the mark is the *name* of the beast and some have demonstrated that the *Arabic* letters which spell "in the name of allah," when turned on their side, are identical, stroke for stroke, to the *Greek* letters for 666. See below.

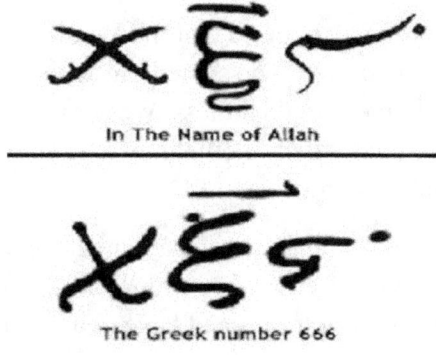

Those are truly identical. And if we take Islam to be equivalent to the religion of the Beast, then the mark is almost literally "in the name of the beast."

The Islamic State issued "repentance cards" to anyone within their territory who agreed to "repent" and submit to Islam and their authority. They issue these not only to former members of other religions, but to policemen, soldiers, teachers, English speakers, and anyone else with any western influence as well.

If ISIS enforcers happen to catch *anyone* who was issued a repentance card but without that card on their person, then they were immediately killed. In such a society, it is no hard stretch of the imagination to believe that the general populace themselves might begin to beg for a permanent mark or tattoo on their hands to prevent the possible loss of their repentance card.

The Failure of the Nations to Stop It

Before Trump, the United States, the UK, France, Russia, Iran, Syria, Iraq, and others all tried to stop ISIS militarily without success. The big guys like the United States, Russia, and Europe hadn't done much of anything beyond dropping some bombs and sending in a few special forces.

Why?

Because while everyone recognized that the Islamic State is evil, many of the politicians with the power to do something actually don't care as much about human rights as they would profess. Western governments are mostly concerned about the production of oil and who is allied with whom in the Middle East to ensure its flow.

When horrific images of massacres play in the media, politicians get pressed and will be moved enough to drop bombs – because bombs just cost money – but to commit troops and have your own countries' families mourning their dead sons and daughters on camera ... well, the conviction just isn't strong enough to provoke that level of commitment.

And the general populations of western nations aren't any better. We see the atrocities played out in excruciating detail daily on TV, but it isn't happening to us. *We* aren't suffering the loss of life, the oppression, the devastation of property and destruction of innocence, so we don't want to send our sons and daughters to help endangered children at the risk of losing our own.

Even when ISIS set off some bombs in New York City or sent a terrorist streaking through a mall in Minnesota to stab as many people as possible, we frowned, but "it didn't happen to *our* family, so we'll just wait for someone in the government to fix it."

This article on a popular blog is worth reading:

http://blogs.berkeley.edu/2015/03/02/how-to-defeat-isis-and-why-it-probably-wont-happen/

The author made a very good case the only way the Islamic State will be finally defeated is through a fully committed ground invasion, but in the same breath, he states why he doesn't think it will happen. Keep in mind, while we have made great inroads, we have not fully defeated ISIS and we still don't have the full commitment for the ground invasion needed.

Most interesting are the comments at the end of the article. The commenters are your typical mashup of the uninformed mixed with a few rational-minded people pressing for others to see reason. They do everything from bemoaning the universal evil of religion (only simple minds lump all religions together this way) to suggesting we launch an army of robot dogs to kill them all.

The common thread through all of their "suggestions," however, is *a complete lack of commitment to sacrifice our own lives to help a foreign people.* Every commenter is committed to laziness and their own comfort. They want to find an effortless, push-button solution that will make ISIS go away.

Remember, the best translation of Daniel 8:25 says, *"through complacency, he shall destroy many."*

The Support of Turkey

In the minds of the public, the Islamic State is just an evil anomaly. A little beast that is murdering wherever it can and many governments are just too inept to stop it while Western powers don't care enough.

But add a little thought to that equation, and some interesting questions rise to the surface. How exactly did a smallish, landlocked "state" make so much money selling oil? They didn't have any seaports, so how did they distribute it with impunity?

The answer is their long, northern border with Turkey. It's no accident the Islamic State's territory is mostly in the northern areas of Syria and Iraq. Through pipelines and trucks, they sold their oil to third parties across the Turkish border in exchange for millions of dollars per day.

And it's not that Turkey is just incompetent to stop this trade, or that they're looking the other way. All of this oil was purchased by the Turkish president's son, Bilal Erdoğan, who then used European-based companies to ship it to Japan and elsewhere.[83]

But that's not all.

President Erdoğan's daughter is directing a secret hospital inside Syria where ISIS fighters are patched up of their wounds and sent back into battle – or presumably this may be the place where organs are being harvested from wounded warriors to be transplanted into rich, sick people who are willing to pay.[84]

Turkey recently shot down a Russian jet that was on a bombing run to blow up one of the ISIS' key oil pipelines. This jet was inside *Syrian* airspace at

---

[83] http://www.breitbart.com/national-security/2015/12/12/Erdoğan-and-the-islamic-state-oil-trade-is-turkey-funding-terrorism/
[84] http://www.mintpressnews.com/211624-2/211624/

the time and had permission from the Syrian government to be there. Mistake? No, this was the Turkish president protecting his son's oil business.[85]

In October, 2014, Vice-president Joe Biden told an audience at Harvard that Erdoğan was supporting ISIS with "hundreds of millions of dollars and thousands of tons of weapons."

Of course, a lot of those weapons were sourced by Turkey from the United States. It also appears ISIS soldiers have even been trained by U.S, Israeli, and Turkish special forces in secret bases in Syria for the past three years.[86]

Why would the United States or Israel even participate in this? Well, it's possible that we were "tricked" into it – that we were told the men being trained belonged to a different group of Syrian rebels when in fact they were ISIS. Unfortunately, some politicians in the Clinton State Department probably had more notorious reasons.

It is also known that many ISIS commanders speak Turkish as their primary language, a very surprising fact given the strong Muslim identity of the terror state.

They should be speaking Arabic unless there is a specific reason why they speak Turkish.

In late 2015, US forces recovered a senior ISIS' commander's cell phone which contained indisputable evidence of his connection to Turkish intelligence agencies and the level of security and protection Turkey is giving ISIS.[87]

As one U.S. official put it, "Turkey's role has not been ambiguous — it has overtly supported the Islamic State. It has provided logistical support, money, weapons, transport and healthcare to wounded warriors."[88]

---

[85] http://www.mintpressnews.com/211624-2/211624/
[86] http://www.mintpressnews.com/211624-2/211624/
[87] http://www.mintpressnews.com/killed-isis-commanders-cell-phone-shows-direct-ties-to-turkish-intelligence/212317/
[88] http://www.mintpressnews.com/killed-isis-commanders-cell-phone-shows-direct-ties-to-turkish-intelligence/212317/

Therefore, given all of the above, it seems very clear the Islamic State is not an independent terror-state, but in fact an arm of the Turkish government protected and controlled by President Erdoğan himself.

Summary

The Islamic State exploded onto the word scene with advanced military strategy, propaganda, financial structure, and governance already well-developed at its birth. This high-level sophistication combined with its incredible funding and successes means it is not reasonable to believe they grew to such heights without significant support from a major power.

Its commanders speak Turkish, are connected to Turkish intelligence officers (they have their phone numbers programmed in their cell phones), cross the Turkish border with impunity, receive training in Turkey, sell their oil to the Turkish president's son for funding, and even receive medical care from his daughter. The Turkish military intervened to stop Russia from hurting ISIS' oil interests, and the U.S. government and others have publicly said Turkey is offering ISIS significant material support.

This means the true leader of ISIS never was Abu Bakr Al-Baghdadi. It is and always has been President Erdoğan of Turkey.

Why would he do this? Why would he launch a terrorist organization such as ISIS, yet cover his involvement with deception?

We will answer those questions soon. For now, let's note that if President Erdoğan is the true leader of ISIS, then what we have seen them commit in the way of atrocities and horrors around the world is a reflection of his heart. It is what he does do and would do if he were completely unfettered by the checks and balances of the Turkish government.

Erdoğan & The Antichrist

The "Failed" Coup

WE BEGAN BY REPORTING the attempted coup in 2016 by the Turkish military to remove Erdoğan from power – *and how it failed.*

The reason the coup was attempted in the first place is that the Turkish military has always viewed itself as the protector of human rights in Turkey. Over recent decades, they have intervened many times to stop any oppressive prime minister who began violating the people's rights.

As one of their generals said, "In Turkey, we have a marriage of Islam and democracy…The child of this marriage is secularism. Now this child gets sick from time to time. The Turkish Armed Forces is the doctor which saves the child. Depending on how sick the kid is, we administer the necessary medicine to make sure the child recuperates."[89]

However, what stood out about the 2016 coup is that this was the only coup in recent Turkish history that was *stopped*. More significantly, it was stopped by the Turkish *president* who isn't supposed to have any control of the government. According to the Turkish constitution, the *prime minister* has all the power.

Erdoğan had previously maxed out his term limits as prime minister, which is why he ran for president, a figurehead position.[90] Upon taking office as president, he immediately and illegally began taking control of the

---

[89] General Çevik Bir, *"Türkiye'de 'Demokrasi Ayarı' Şart!"*. *Kibrispostasi.com.* 28 February 2007.
[90] http://www.reuters.com/article/us-turkey-election-idUSBREA410U820140502

government again and forced the actual prime minister to resign under some unknown threat.[91]

Thus, the military decided to intervene. The swiftness with which Erdoğan put down this coup (led by the leaders of a very strong military) struck many observers as highly odd. This would be like the Pentagon moving to remove Trump from office, but Trump somehow stopping the Pentagon using primarily civilian militias in just twenty-four hours! It is believed by many that what actually happened is Erdoğan engineered his own coup in order to discover who in the army would be against him so he could cull them out.[92]

Erdoğan is a very strong Islamist and believes Turkey should be ruled by Sharia law.[93] It would appear that he sent agents into his own army to instigate a coup against himself that he was ready to stop so he could have an excuse to eliminate anyone who would oppose him from every aspect of society: military, government, courts, schools, universities, professionals, business, and media.

Could Erdoğan Be the Antichrist?

If the Islamic State is a precursor of the Beast, and Erdoğan is its shadowy father, then it's a no brainer that we should evaluate this president of Turkey as a potential candidate for the antichrist.

> *"Little children, it is the last hour; and as you have heard that the Antichrist is coming, even now many antichrists have come, by which we know that it is the last hour ... Who is a liar but he who denies that Jesus is the Christ?*

---

[91] http://www.npr.org/sections/thetwo-way/2016/05/05/476856576/turkeys-prime-minister-to-step-down-as-president-Erdoğan-pushes-for-more-power
[92] https://www.theguardian.com/world/2016/jul/16/fethullah-gulen-turkey-coup-Erdoğan
[93] http://www.al-monitor.com/pulse/originals/2016/04/turkey-does-Erdoğan-aim-islamic-state.html

He is antichrist who denies the Father and the Son. Whoever denies the Son does not have the Father either; he who acknowledges the Son has the Father also."
(1 John 2: 18, 22-23)

The Book of 1 John teaches that there have been many antichrists in history. The definition of *an* antichrist is whether or not they have the spirit of the antichrist, which is a spirit that acts and teaches the opposite of what Jesus did and taught. Hitler was an example of an antichrist.

These lower-case "antichrists" are distinct from *the* antichrist, the last and worst of all of them to come right before the true Christ (Messiah) returns.

So, first question: Does Erdoğan have the spirit of the antichrist?

As a hardline Islamist, Erdoğan very publicly and forcefully denies that Jesus is God's Son. According to 1 John 2, that is enough to qualify him as an antichrist. (John is not saying that everyday people who haven't yet recognized Jesus as Messiah are "antichrists," he is referring to "activists" who actively work against and deny Jesus.)

Jesus is Lord of the universe, master of all eternity, and yet when He came to earth to live among us, He chose to be born in a lowly animal enclosure with a feeding trough for His cradle. He never clamored for attention, never demanded worship. He served and loved the lowliest members of society and died to save those who hated Him. In everything, He had every right to rule, yet in everything, He showed humility.

In contrast, during an October, 2015 meeting, the president of the European Commission, Jean-Claude Juncker, complained to Erdoğan about his hardline stance on the refugee crisis, saying "didn't we treat you like a prince during your last visit?" To which Erdoğan reacted furiously. *"Like a prince?* Of course, I'm not representing a third world country."

That arrogance, self-importance, entitled demand for others to serve him is the opposite of the spirit of Christ.

Jesus' many healings and loving words are well-known. He not only taught us to turn the other cheek, but He lived it out, asking God from the cross to forgive those who had crucified Him.

Yet, Erdoğan imprisons, tortures, and murders anyone who would stand or speak against him.

Jesus showed love to the Samaritans, a race hated by other Jews in His time.

Oppositely, Erdoğan is very racist and has repeatedly expressed a deep-seated hatred for the Kurds, Armenians, Jews, and other races.[94]

It seems clear that Erdoğan is *an* antichrist in that he is full of the spirit of the antichrist. So, now the question becomes: Is Erdoğan *the* antichrist?

---

[94] https://sputniknews.com/middleeast/20160209/1034477022/turkey-Erdoğan-kurdophobia-crackdown-kurds.html

Erdoğan Openly Admires Hitler

Erdoğan has said he admires Hitler and intends to model his new Turkey after Hitler's Germany.[95] Unfortunately, the response of most westerners to these comments was to laugh and mock rather than recognize the threat for what it was.

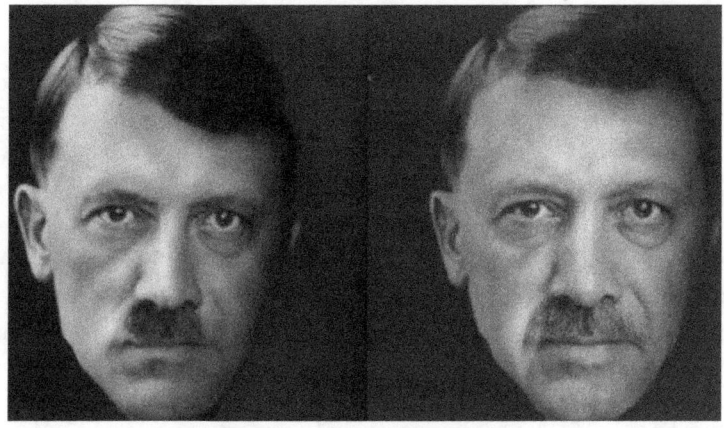

Erdoğan even looks like Hitler. Related?

Erdoğan has repeatedly expressed extreme hatred for Armenians and Kurds and implies he would like to use solutions against them like Hitler's persecution of the Jewish people.

---

[95] http://www.al-monitor.com/pulse/originals/2016/04/turkey-does-Erdoğan-aim-islamic-state.html

Erdoğan is Arrogant and Boastful

"And there, in this horn, were eyes like the eyes of a man, and a mouth speaking pompous words." (Daniel 7:8)

The little "horn" in that passage is commonly understood to be referring to the antichrist. Pompous words will define him.

A listener would be hard-pressed to attend an Erdoğan speech without hearing brashness, arrogance, and pride.[96] He commonly refers to other races as being beneath himself and the Turks. He routinely refers to the greatness of Turkey and how it will save Europe from itself and show it the right way of doing things.

He demands to be treated like royalty wherever he goes, believes the ultimate sin would be for himself or Turkey to ever bow their head to anyone,[97] and has a special hatred for those who would try to humble him.

Truly, Erdoğan's pompous and prideful spirit is the opposite of Christ.

---

[96] http://www.thecaliforniacourier.com/who-is-responsible-for-turning-Erdoğan-into-a-fanatical-tyrant/
[97] http://www.thecaliforniacourier.com/who-is-responsible-for-turning-Erdoğan-into-a-fanatical-tyrant/

Erdoğan Is Starting to Claim Divinity

"Let no one deceive you by any means; for that Day will not come unless the falling away comes first, and the man of sin is revealed, the son of perdition, who opposes and exalts himself above all that is called God or that is worshiped, so that he sits as God in the temple of God, showing himself that he is God." (2 Thessalonians 2:3-4)

The antichrist will eventually elevate himself above God and even claim to be God himself.

Interestingly, members of Erdoğan's political party and Muslim clerics have begun using vocabulary and phrases to describe Erdoğan that until now have only been used to refer to the prophet Mohammad or Allah.

Erdoğan himself has begun to speak of himself in divine terms, using phrases that are spoken only by Allah in Muslim scriptures,[98] and he has imprisoned Muslim clerics who have challenged him for doing so.

While these claims to divinity are somewhat "mild" at this point, if he is saying such things before he has even begun to conquer, it is no stretch at all to believe that before he is done the blasphemy will become outrageous.

His Name Adds Up

*"He causes all, both small and great, rich and poor, free and slave, to receive a mark on their right hand or on their foreheads, and that no one may buy or sell except one who has the mark or the name of the beast, or **the number of his name.***

---

[98] http://shoebat.com/2015/03/31/shocking-and-amazing-Erdoğan-has-now-declared-himself-to-be-god/

> *Here is wisdom.* **Let him who has understanding calculate the number of the beast**, *for it is the number of a man: His number is 666."*
> *(Revelation 13:16-18)*

Every Greek letter has a number value, similar to Roman numerals. In Ancient Greece, they had no numbers, they simply repurposed letters for mathematical calculations. So, every early believer reading a Greek word could read it both as a word, or as a number.

As we said earlier, Jesus' name in Greek adds up to 888. Every early believer would have known that and seen it easily.

1	α	alpha	10	ι	iota	100	ρ	rho
2	β	beta	20	κ	kappa	200	σ	sigma
3	γ	gamma	30	λ	lambda	300	τ	tau
4	δ	delta	40	μ	mu	400	υ	upsilon
5	ε	epsilon	50	ν	nu	500	φ	phi
6	ϛ	vau*	60	ξ	xi	600	χ	chi
7	ζ	zeta	70	ο	omicron	700	ψ	psi
8	η	eta	80	π	pi	800	ω	omega
9	θ	theta	90	ϙ	koppa*	900	ϡ	sampi

*vau, koppa, and sampi are obsolete characters

Jesus

Ἰησοῦς

$(10+8+200+70+400+200 = 888)$

Therefore, when Revelation 13 says that he who has wisdom should calculate the number of the beast, it is teaching us that the antichrist's name in Greek will add up to 666.

Recent events in the Middle East prompted this author to test the name of the current president of Turkey with this criteria:

Tayyip	Erdoğan (Turkish spelling)
Ταγίπ	Ερντογάν (Modern Greek spelling)
(300+1+3+10+80 = 394)	(5+100+50+300+70+3+1+50 = 579)

However, the Turkish "ğ" is *not* a hard "g" sound like the English "g," nor does it sound like the Greek "gamma" (which is used in the calculation above).

The Turkish "ğ" is a swallowed vowel sound that corresponds to the ancient and no-longer-used Greek letter "Qoppa" (Koppa), from which comes the English "q" and the Arabic "Qaf". In Syria, Lebanon, Israel, and Egypt, the Arabic letter "Qaf" has the exact same swallowed vowel sound that the Turkish "ğ" has.

Therefore, the most accurate Greek spelling of the Turkish president's name is:

Ταϱίπ	**Ερντοϱάν** (Ancient Greek spelling)
(300+1+90+10+80 = 481)	(5+100+50+300+70+90+1+50 = **666**)

Now, does this prove that Erdoğan is absolutely the antichrist? No, not by itself.

However, we will say that in 20 years of testing names, no matter who or what name was tested and tried using this system, this author has never had any other name previously add up to the exact sum of 666.

Combine that with the fact that Erdoğan is a violent oppressor of his people, a fanatical Muslim and egotist (not in that order), and has been exposed recently as the founder, financier, and trainer of ISIS, and the evidence becomes quite startling that he may indeed be the evil one long foretold.

Especially considering he has *begun* the conquest of three nations, and the Prophet Daniel said the antichrist would conquer three nations.

ZACK MASON

He Will Conquer Three Nations

Doing an internet search for "characteristics of the antichrist" reveals the wide variety of crazy opinions on the subject. The top results are pages pronouncing the antichrist to be Barack Obama, the Pope, and even Prince Charles of England (That last one is just funny – what does anyone have against Prince Charles?)

It's disappointing to see so many people dedicating serious brain power to deciphering prophecy without actually thinking about what they're doing. (Or it could be argued that Google is conspiring to keep the dumbest blogs at the top of their results to discredit Christians who are serious students of prophecy – it's already been proven that Google has is doing such things in the political realm ...)

There are well-established principles of biblical interpretation that must always be followed (even by bloggers) including and especially with the interpretation of prophecy, such as:

- Respecting the author's original intent
- Understanding the historical context
- Keeping in mind the intended audience
- Respecting the type of literature
- And more

When Old Testament prophets call the antichrist "the Assyrian," it is hard to see how any serious student of prophecy could twist and stretch those words to somehow symbolically implicate Prince Charles or the Pope. Why wouldn't the antichrist just actually be Assyrian?

It's also disappointing to see so many of the online commenters joking and mocking and showing no fear of the Word of God. When God dedicates significant space in Scripture to a subject, we do well to pay attention to it.

"After this I saw in the night visions, and behold, a fourth beast, dreadful and terrible, exceedingly strong. It had

> *huge iron teeth; it was devouring, breaking in pieces, and trampling the residue with its feet. It was different from all the beasts that were before it,* **and it had ten horns***. I was considering the horns,* **and there was another horn***, a little one, coming up among them,* **before whom three of the first horns were plucked out by the roots***. And there, in this horn, were eyes like the eyes of a man, and a mouth speaking pompous words."*
> (Daniel 7:8)

Daniel's prediction above is universally recognized as referring to the antichrist. The little horn is the antichrist, and he rises up among a group of other kings and conquers three of them.

In the prophecy, there are seven more "horns" that also come under the authority of the antichrist and "rule with him for an hour." So, we should expect that since violence is described for only three of the nations, that the other seven come under his authority voluntarily.

Which Nations Will Be the Three?

There are a total number of 10 nations in the coalition described by Daniel. This is the same number stated in the Book of Revelation.

Another prophetic passage, Psalm 83, which is a psalm predicting a future war, lists 10 nations by name that come together in a coalition for a future attack on Israel.

> *"O God, do not remain silent;*
> *do not turn a deaf ear,*
> *do not stand aloof, O God.*
> *See how your enemies growl,*
> *how your foes rear their heads.*
>
> *With cunning they conspire against your people;*
> *they plot against those you cherish.*

> *"Come," they say, "let us destroy them as a nation,*
> *so that Israel's name is remembered no more."*
>
> *With one mind they plot together;*
> *they form an alliance against you—*
> *the tents of Edom and the Ishmaelites,*
> *of Moab and the Hagrites,*
> *Byblos [Gebal], Ammon and Amalek,*
> *Philistia, with the people of Tyre.*
> *Even Assyria has joined them to reinforce Lot's descendants."*
> *(Psalm 83:1-8, NIV)*

These nations today are all Muslim neighbors surrounding Israel and are the same nations destined for a special judgment by God in the last days according to the Books of Isaiah, Jeremiah, Ezekiel, and others.

Within that coalition, Psalm 83:8 singles Assyria out in its language from the other nine peoples:

"Even Assyria has joined them to reinforce Lot's descendants."

That can mean that Assyria joins them as in it becomes a part of their coalition – or it can mean that Assyria *joins* them as in Assyria is the leader who forms the coalition and unites the others together in an effort to help "the children of Lot." (The children of Lot today are known as the West Bank Palestinians and other Jordanians.)

If you don't know much about the political situation in Israel currently, we should explain that there are two different groups of self-described Palestinians living in the land of Israel today who claim the land is theirs instead of Israel.

Historically, their claim is not valid, and there is very little evidence of their presence in the land until the Jews started returning in the early 1900's, not to mention that God covenanted the land to Abraham and his descendants (Israel) four *thousand* years ago.

In truth, the conflict is more about pride and the general Muslim hate for the Jewish people than anything else, and this hatred has driven the Palestinians to commit countless atrocities and acts of terror against Jews in Israel and around the world.

Technically, only one of the groups are actually "Palestinians," *the ones that live in the southern coastal Gaza Strip.*

These are the original *Philistines* (Change the "p" to a "ph" and you've got *Phalestinians*) that Israel has been fighting all the way back since Old Testament times. And they're still living in the same cities where they've always lived.

The second group of modern "Palestinians," a much larger group, occupies the majority of the territory known as the West Bank that butts right up against the nation of Jordan to the East. These hills are the traditional land that Israel occupied in Old Testament times. Therefore, if any land is theirs by right, it is that land.

For those who believe the West Bank Palestinians lived there for centuries and are being uprooted by modern-day Jewish immigration, we recommend doing a little more in-depth research regarding the matter. The truth is that before Jewish immigration, the land of the West Bank had become largely desolate and uninhabited. Jordanian Muslims began moving there *in response to Jewish migration*. They saw that Jews were moving in, planting trees, rehabilitating mismanaged land, and restoring it to an arable state, so they moved in to take advantage of the change and because they were outraged by a returned Jewish presence in the Middle East (which could not be allowed).[99]

Twice the Arab Muslims joined together to try and expel the Jewish people but were defeated both times. After that, they adopted different techniques (terrorism and deceitful political claims) to continue the struggle. They've

---

[99] https://www.conservativereview.com/news/the-truth-about-palestine/

continually done this in violation of legal U.N. resolutions granting Israel a lot more land than they hold today.

Today, these West Bank "Palestinians" stubbornly hold on and refuse to return the land that belongs to Israel rightfully, and they even occupy the Temple Mount, the holiest spot in both the Jewish and Christian faiths and refuse to let Jews pray there.

Genetically speaking, these inhabitants of the West Bank are not actually Palestinians, but Jordanians. And Jordanians are the Children of Lot.

The ancient peoples listed in Psalm 83 correspond to modern day nations of Turkey, Saudi Arabia, Egypt, Jordan, the Gaza Strip, and Hezbollah in Southern Lebanon. Two important places *not* listed are Syria (Aram) and Iraq (Babylon). This is very curious, especially Syria since it lies between Turkey and Israel and a presumed Turkish invasion of Israel would be very difficult without the participation of Syria.

Regardless, there would seem to be only two possible explanations. Either Syria and Iraq will not be angry enough at Israel to join the coalition (unlikely), or *they are no longer independent entities from Assyria (Turkey) at that time.*

Also not mentioned is Iran (Persia). Modern-day Iran is a virulent enemy of Turkey and unlikely to join any confederation led by them, so if Erdoğan is the antichrist, this absence also makes sense.

As we consider the ten-horned Beast described in Daniel and Revelation and compare it with Psalm 83, the best interpretation in our opinion is a world scene where Turkey conquers Syria and Iraq by force (and one other nation) in the name of establishing an Islamic Caliphate, essentially recreating the ancient borders of the Assyrian Empire. Then, seven other Middle Eastern nations (ethnic groups) would sign a treaty with the New Assyria to form a coalition for the sole purpose of destroying Israel *"as a nation, so that Israel's name is remembered no more."* (Psalm 83:4)

So, Psalm 83 gives us a good idea which nations will comprise the future Islamic Caliphate, and it gives us hints as to which countries might be among the three conquered by the antichrist. According to the prophet Daniel, that conquest of three nations is one of the primary identifiers of the antichrist.

So…Does Erdoğan Fit?

The Little Horn

"And out of one of them came a little horn which grew exceedingly great toward the south, toward the east, and toward the Glorious Land." (Daniel 8:9)

"While I was thinking about the horns, there before me was another horn, a little one, which came up among them; and three of the first horns were uprooted before it. This horn had eyes like the eyes of a human being and a mouth that spoke boastfully." (Daniel 7:8)

It is this author's belief that July 15th, 2016 may possibly be the day the Lamb of God *began* breaking the 1st seal of the scroll of Revelation.

NOTE: In our minds, we might expect Jesus breaking a seal in Heaven to have a sudden and monumental impact on the world. However, the Bible says that "one day is like a thousand years unto the Lord." (2 Peter 3:8) Therefore, for us, it could be like Jesus is breaking the seal in severe slow-motion. We should not expect immediate, sudden impact, but a slower build-up. For example, in the Book of Revelation, a rider on a red horse rides out (2nd seal) which represents war. Yet, it seems obvious that war will not immediately break out that day. Instead, we'll see an unrelenting build-up of anger, smaller antagonisms and maybe even skirmishes, until a full-blown war actually begins.

A horseman does not ride for a few paces only, but he rides along a path, and it seems reasonable to say that the antagonisms between nations would not begin until the horseman has actually begun riding. Some readers might be wondering if the horsemen aren't just literary symbols? The answer is no. Yes, they are symbolic in a sense, but they are actual spiritual beings that John witnessed while in Heaven whose actions provoke historical events here on earth during the end times. (The Bible repeatedly says that earthly history is directed by happenings in the spiritual realm.)

Some might argue that since Erdoğan was already the President of Turkey, he did not conquer Turkey. But this is honestly not true. As *president* he had no political power, nor control over the military. He was supposed to be a figurehead, kind of like the Queen of England.

When he was running for president, many warned him that he would not be allowed to seek to hold actual political power while holding that office.

Before the coup, all military and executive powers in Turkey were constitutionally held with the office of the prime minister, *not the president.*

But after winning the election for the figurehead position, Erdoğan forced Turkey's duly elected prime minister to resign, then declared himself to be in absolute control and conquered the Turkish military as they tried to remove him. He then proceeded to pluck his opposition "out by the roots."

However, since Erdoğan currently has tanks and troops in three countries and is slowly "conquering" there, we feel the coup in Turkey most likely represents the little horn rising "up among them."

The First Horn

Under the guise of fighting the Islamic State, Erdoğan has sent soldiers and tanks across the border into Syria.[100] By September of 2016, for instance, Turkish forces had "taken" 17 villages from ISIS.

Al Jazeera, an Arabic news source like CNN, reported some intriguing statements made by eyewitnesses on the initial Turkish incursion:

> ***"There are no clashes**, ISIS fighters flee as soon as they see us advancing, especially because we are supported by Turkish air power."*

> *"**Turkish tanks have not entered any of the villages** but have remained on standby on the Syrian side of the border."*

Al Jazeera further reported:

> *"[The] operation was Ankara's most ambitious during the five-and-a-half-year Syria conflict, and has since continued with tanks, fighter jets and special forces providing support to rebels."*

Since then, Turkey has slowly kept increasing the Syrian territory it holds and now it *is* entering cities.[101] Turkey's entire stated reason for invading northern Syria was to fight ISIS, yet to date they have done battle against every force in Syria *except* ISIS and steadily refused to engage the forces of the Islamic State.

---

[100] http://www.aljazeera.com/news/2016/09/syria-turkish-backed-rebels-seize-isil-territory-160903131731273.html
[101] https://www.nytimes.com/2018/03/22/world/middleeast/turkey-syria-afrin.html

Knowing the real power is behind the Islamic State, the Syrian government has formed a strong alliance with Russia and is allowing Russian jets and troops to operate within its borders against ISIS.

American forces, presumably in the country to support Turkey and "democracy," were "tricked" by supposedly friendly forces into bombing Syrian government forces at key moments thinking they were ISIS. Sad to say, Western (especially European) politicians don't seem to care as much about the freedom of your average Syrian or whether Christians are being massacred as much as they want inexpensive oil. Cheap oil is considered a matter of national security for Europe. And they dearly want to diminish the influence of Russia.

Those that would be called "globalists" in Western politics want Turkey to establish an Islamic Caliphate. They believe that this will accomplish many "good" things. They believe the establishment of a Turkish Islamic Caliphate over Syria and Iraq will:

- Create more stability in the Middle East
- End Islamic State terrorist attacks in Europe
- Severely diminish the influence of Russia and Iran on the Middle East
- Create a strong Muslim power to counterbalance Israel
- Force Israel into peace negotiations
- Allow the construction of a major oil pipeline extending from Qatar, across the Caliphate, and into Europe
- End Europe's dependence on Russian oil

It is unclear at this juncture how serious the push against Russia will be, but the end result looks likely to be a final confrontation between Turkey and Syria, with Turkey winning and beginning a press toward Damascus.

What is clear is that Turkey has no intention of leaving. After 5 years, they continue to hold territory in Syria long after ISIS evaporated. In early 2020, Turkey shot down 2 Syrian military planes and destroyed over 100 tanks and 6 air defense systems.¹⁰² This is the beginning of a sustained military offensive against the Syrian government.

The purpose of ISIS now has become clear. It was always designed to enter into Muslim nations Erdoğan wished to conquer and destabilize them pre-emptively. Once ISIS destabilized the country, weakened the government, created chaos, and made the world hate them, Erdoğan entered with his military to establish order and "protect" people.

Yet, wherever the Turkish military goes, ISIS simply melts away as they are comrades in arms. In fact, ISIS had always prophesied about themselves that they would not last but were being used for a purpose. Of course, once the Turkish army arrives on the scene, that army doesn't leave.

The Second Horn

In late 2015, Turkey also began secretly moving soldiers and tanks into Northern Iraq. Their stated purpose was to fight ISIS from the north in aid of Baghdad. However, Baghdad said they did not invite Turkey into the country and wanted them to leave immediately.¹⁰³

Inside Iraq, at first it did not seem that Turkish forces were really doing much of anything. They just infiltrated a few thousand soldiers along with a good number of tanks and sat themselves outside of the City of Mosul (anciently called Ninevah, once capital of Assyria). From there, they occasionally tossed an ineffective shell toward the insurgents for effect, but that was about it.

Any objective, outside observer would have said they were occupying territory and waiting for something.

---

[102] https://www.dailymail.co.uk/news/article-8062327/Turkey-shoots-two-Syrian-war-planes-destroys-100-tanks-launches-military-offensive.html
[103] http://www.telegraph.co.uk/news/worldnews/islamic-state/12172521/Turkish-troops-taking-on-Isil-in-secret-battle-in-Iraq.html

Then, in 2018, Erdoğan announced he was ordering his military to launch new operations in Northern Iraq to conquer the area of Sinjar (*Shinar* in the Bible).[104] The original mission of fighting ISIS morphed into killing Kurds, a people that is most likely descended from one of the lost tribes of Israel.

Since June 2018, Erdoğan has doubled his military presence in Northern Iraq and established at least 11 military bases there to fight the Kurds.[105] His operations against the Kurds and the taking of more territory continues to increase.[106]

Erdoğan is potentially about to conquer two nations through very deceptive means – *and these two potential conquests are exactly the two nations we have identified as the most probable candidates to fulfill biblical prophecy.*

In addition, from Daniel 8:25 we know that the antichrist will cause "deceit to prosper," and Erdoğan is clearly using deception to prosper.

The Third Horn

Since 2014, a civil war in Libya has been raging, called by many the *Second Libyan Civil War*. The war is between various factions, but primarily between the duly elected House of Representatives on one side and the Prime Minister Fayez al-Sarraj on the other.

In the beginning of 2020, Turkey joined the fight by sending troops and other military forces to Libya.[107] Their stated goal is to assist the "Government of National Accord" (the Prime Minister's army) against the House of Representatives. Turkey is professing to be legally supporting the

---

[104] https://www.telegraph.co.uk/news/2018/03/25/turkey-begins-operation-iraqs-sinjar-Erdoğan-says/
[105] http://www.breitbart.com/national-security/2018/06/04/turkeys-military-activities-iraq-soaring-11-bases-troop-presence-doubled/
[106] https://apnews.com/4dd4686c4c62e3bd978cc34901ca87a4
[107] https://en.wikipedia.org/wiki/Turkish_military_intervention_in_the_Second_Libyan_Civil_War

legal government of Libya. Of course, they have many interests beyond that, from economic to geopolitical.[108]

Before Turkey's strong involvement, the prime minister's forces had been reduced to a small area around Tripoli on the coast. However, with Turkey's support, in just a few months, that changed to the point where at the time of this writing, Turkish troops control almost the entire western half of the country.

It seems clear Turkey will win this war. No one in the west cares enough about Libya to spend much time studying the factions, much less trying to get people passionate about one side or the other. All the West remembers about Libya is Gaddafi and the bombing of Flight 103. We've written Libya off, we frankly don't care who rules it, and the Libyan House of Representatives does not have the resources to fight Turkey off. Only with outside help from Russia or Saudi Arabia and Egypt could they hope to prevail.

In fact, in fear of Turkey's moves, Egypt is threatening to invade Libya to stop them.[109] Will it happen? Probably not. After the initial threat, Egypt then said it would only move in troops to protect its western border if it became necessary. Translation: There isn't enough political will inside Egypt to go to war with Turkey over Libya.

It is important to remember that Erdoğan does not have the humility of George Washington. Turkey is not the United States. When it wins, they will not just keep a few bases in a country to maintain peace as the U.S. has always done. No, when they win, Turkey will make it clear they are the ones who rule, not the Libyan prime minister in whose name they have come to help.

After Syria and Iraq both fall as well, Turkey will move to unite all of its conquests under the banner of the Islamic superpower, the Caliphate.

---

[108] https://www.dw.com/en/what-is-turkey-doing-in-libya/a-49505173
[109] https://www.breitbart.com/national-security/2020/06/25/egypt-threatens-invasion-libya-stop-turkey/

Other Options

The nations of Armenia and Azerbaijan in the Caucasus mountains have been fighting over territory. In July of 2020, Erdoğan announced he would be sending materiel support to Azerbaijan in its fight against Armenia, including drones, missiles and air defense systems.[110] He called Armenia (a people he hates and again a probable lost tribe of Israel) an "invader".

If he were to conquer Armenia in the name of helping Azerbaijan, and Azerbaijan were a strong partner, Erdoğan would have access to the Caspian Sea as well as the Black and Mediterranean seas, a major coup. See the map below:

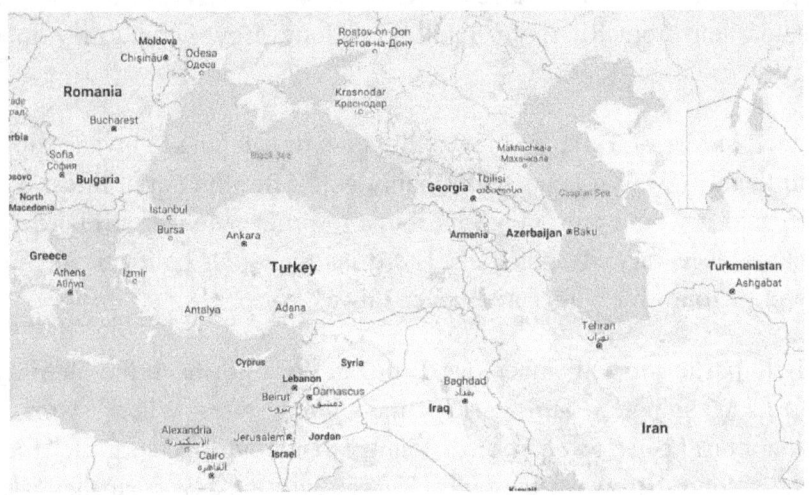

Source: Google Maps

If he accomplished this, it would allow him to exert tremendous pressure on Russia, Iran, and otherwise landlocked countries in Asia. An aggressive

---

[110] https://www.bloomberg.com/news/articles/2020-07-17/Erdoğan-offers-to-aid-azerbaijan-after-skirmishes-with-armenia

Turkey could become the gateway to the Mediterranean for many countries and strongly control shipping lanes.

Of note, Armenia is a Christian country sandwiched between Muslim Turkey and Muslim Azerbaijan.

So, Armenia could be the third horn instead of one of the others. Or it could be another nation he has not yet invaded.

However, if Erdoğan is the antichrist, he will conquer three nations and seven more will enter the Caliphate voluntarily. That specific combo is what we are watching for.

Who Are the Other Seven?

This is unknown, but being Muslim and geographically close to Turkey would be the most important characteristics. Based on that criteria, these are the most probable:

- Egypt
- Saudi Arabia
- Yemen
- Oman
- Qatar
- United Arab Emirates
- Bahrain
- Kuwait
- Jordan
- Azerbaijan
- Lebanon
- Sudan

That is twelve nations, not seven, so the initial Caliphate would not include all of these. Due to different prophecies that indicate Jordan *might* not be a part of the Caliphate, this author considers it less likely. Time will tell!

The Antichrist Will Not Share the Religion of His Ancestors

> *"He will show no regard for the gods of his ancestors or for the one desired by women, nor will he regard any god, but will exalt himself above them all." (Daniel 11:37, NIV)*

When Daniel wrote that passage, he was immersed in pagan Persia (modern day Iran). The Persian king, the Persian governors and the Persian nobility surrounding him were all polytheists. Like modern Hindus and the ancient Romans, they worshipped a wide variety of idols. Their gods were numerous, some minor, some major.

The people of Babylon and Assyria were no different. In fact, when it comes to religious beliefs, all of these ancient cultures were much more similar to each other than you might realize. Their major gods were really the same gods. Their names changed from people to people, but the myth stories were similar.

Daniel is writing of a future Assyrian antichrist, so when he says, "*He will show no regard for the gods of his ancestors,*" Daniel is referring to the ancient pagan gods of Assyria. He is *not* saying that the antichrist will invent a new religion. In other words, he is not saying the antichrist will necessarily break with the religion of his father and grandfather, but with the religion of his ancestors, which were the pagan gods of Daniel's day.

Daniel finishes the sentence by saying, "*[he] will exalt himself above them all [gods].*" As we pointed out earlier, Erdoğan of Turkey (ancient Assyria) is beginning to refer to himself in divine terms.

The Antichrist Will Have No Regard for the Desire of Women

The middle of Daniel 11:37 says, *"He will show no regard...for the one desired by women."* Other translations say, "the desires of women" or "the desire of women."

Because of those secondary translations, this part of the verse has been used to promote the idea that the antichrist will be homosexual, or asexual, or that he will abuse women.

Yet, the best translation is in fact the one cited above. Daniel 11:37 has four parts:

> *"He will show no regard for the gods of his ancestors or for the one desired by women, nor will he regard any god, but will exalt himself above them all." (Daniel 11:37, NIV)*

Notice that the first part says the antichrist will not regard the gods of his ancestors, and the third and last parts also pertain to worship and pagan idols. The second part, sandwiched between all those, is the phrase about not regarding "the desire of women" or "the one desired by women." Therefore, it stands to reason that this is not referring to homosexuality, but somehow to pagan gods as that is the theme of the whole verse.

In fact, the Hebrew word used for "desire" here *never* refers to sexual desire, only an emotional longing for something.

In ancient Assyria, they worshipped a god named Tammuz. Tammuz was considered to be a handsome young god who had been killed and whose return from the dead was greatly desired. The primary ritual of the worship of this false god was that at a specific time every year all the women of the nation would gather to weep and mourn over the death of Tammuz and long for his return.

This pagan worship was so prevalent in the ancient Middle East that the prophet Ezekiel (contemporary with Daniel) documents that it had even infected Israel. Ezekiel says that Jewish women sinned against God by weeping for Tammuz outside the gate of God's Temple.

So, it is no stretch to think that "the desire of women" or "the one desired by women" could be a common ancient nickname for Tammuz, and that Daniel never stops referring to pagan gods in 11:37.

That said, since the antichrist will truly be the son of the devil just as Jesus is the Son of God, we can be sure that the antichrist will engage in *every single sin possible.*

We can say with confidence that he will not enjoy normal sexual relations with a wife who fulfills him.

No, he will definitely partake in homosexuality, he will rape, he will be a pedophile, he will likely even engage in acts of bestiality. These things may not be public when he does them, but he will do them, or he wouldn't really be the biggest sinner of all time.

Sufism and Erdoğan

Turkey is known for a special brand of Islam called Sufism. You may have heard the term "whirling dervishes?" This comes from a Sufi practice of spinning in circles until you fall into a trance in an effort to connect with the cosmos or the mysteries of Allah. This is the entire focus of Sufism, to engage in mystical rituals designed to achieve a spiritual transcendence where one can encounter the depths of Allah.

After World War I, with the Ottoman Empire no more, the first President of Turkey, Mustafa Ataturk, established a fully secular government and worked to suppress the influences of Sufism as he modernized his country.

And he was successful! Since then, Turkey has been a uniquely secular and modern nation among its Muslim neighbors … at least until the arrival of Erdoğan. Erdoğan has proclaimed himself to be a follower of Sufism, and specifically a follower of the teachings of the founder of one of Sufism's main orders, Jalal ad-Din Rumi.[111]

Rumi was a Persian poet and theologian. He is noted for several teachings and practices that distinguish it from other branches of Islam, all of which are important for our discussion here.

First, he put a large emphasis on a mystical connection with the cosmos through mystic rituals in order to experience the mysteries of Allah. This sounds eerily close to something Jesus said in Revelation to the church in Thyatira, a church located in Turkey:

> *"Now to you I say, and to the rest in Thyatira, as many as do not have this doctrine, **who have not known the depths of Satan,** as they say, I will put on you no other burden."* (Revelation 2:24)

Jesus is referring to something we have lost knowledge of today, but He does not approve of it and it sounds very close to the language used by Sufis.

Beyond that, Rumi taught that it was okay to declare oneself to be God, and that to do so was the ultimate expression of humility.[112] This teaching is known as the *Fana* in Sufism. Of course, if Erdoğan admires Rumi and is a Sufi, it is no stretch to expect him to not only continue to declare himself to be God, but to increase his blasphemous words.

Lastly, and most disturbingly, Rumi was a severe pedophile, and like many medieval Persian poets, his poetry celebrated in grand ways sex with young boys as the highest form of love.[113] In fact, it appears Sufis developed a practice called the *Sema* in which a group of Sufi men surround a young

---

[111] https://en.trend.az/world/turkey/2345091.html
[112] http://shoebat.com/2014/12/19/new-discovery-Erdoğan-now-reviving-religion-antichrist-will-enable-islamic-mahdi-declare-god/
[113] https://ahvalnews.com/turkey/turkish-journalist-condemns-persian-poet-rumi-over-child-abuse

boy and stare at him intensely until they fall into some kind of lustful trance.[114]

It is a factual statement to say that if Erdoğan embraces Rumi and Sufism, then he is by definition embracing these mystical rituals, pedophilia, and the belief that he can call himself God.

He Will Try to Change the Calendar

> *"He shall speak pompous words against the Most High, shall persecute the saints of the Most High,* **and shall intend to change times and law***. Then the saints shall be given into his hand for a time and times and half a time."* (Daniel 7:25)

One of the characteristics of the antichrist is that he will attempt to change the calendar – the way time is measured throughout his empire, and maybe the world.

In what ways could he change the calendar?

Changing the number of hours in the day, or minutes in the hour would be near impossible. The earth rotates at a constant speed and humanity is very used to the 24-hour cycle. Changing the number of hours would be a very hard battle to fight psychologically.

On the other end of the spectrum, he could simply add new holidays or prohibit the celebration of others. This wouldn't require much effort on his part at all, just an edict. Yet, since holy days vary from country to country as it is, such a change doesn't seem like it would merit a mention in Scripture. No, the changes would have to be more fundamental than that.

---

[114] http://shoebat.com/2015/05/23/Erdoğan-the-leader-of-the-antichrist-nation-of-turkey-confirmed-to-be-a-part-of-a-strange-homosexual-cult/

He could change the number of days in a week. It has been proposed that he would create a 10-day work week instead of 7. It is this author's opinion that such a change would also be too traumatic for people to accept psychologically, though it could theoretically be done. Such a change would be a direct attack on the Sabbath Day established by God.

However, there is one potential change that makes perfect sense and is more doable. Islam has its own calendar that calculates its years based on the life of Mohammad instead of the Birth of Christ. According to Muslims, the world is currently in the year 1438, or 1444, depending on which country is doing the calculating.

Interestingly, Muslim prophecy also says the mahdi will be revealed in the 1440's.

It seems very clear that *if* the antichrist were Islamic, and *especially* if he were the leader of an Islamic Caliphate, that he would demand all year designations in government and business documents to stop being based on the Birth of Christ and instead adopt the Islamic calendar year.

Of course, that would also likely involve the changing of the months to a lunar calendar in accordance with the Islamic calendar. An Islamic antichrist lends itself to an easy fulfillment of this prophecy as he would also push for the adoption of Sharia law.

The Antichrist Will Do as He Pleases

> *"The king will do as he pleases. He will exalt and magnify himself above every god and will say unheard-of things against the God of gods. He will be successful until the time of wrath is completed, for what has been determined must take place."*
> *(Daniel 11:36)*

Erdoğan currently lives in the biggest house in the world.

The new Presidential Palace in Turkey (which Erdoğan built for himself) is a perfect display of Erdoğan's arrogance, self-worship, and lawlessness all at once. With a construction cost of more than one *billion* dollars and over 1,100 rooms decked out in luxurious marble and gold, *it is the largest and costliest house in the world.*

Its construction was also *illegal*.

Erdoğan placed it in the middle of a protected nature reserve in Turkey. In March of 2014, high-level Turkish courts ordered the suspension of the palace's construction even as he belligerently continued to build his mansion. The revoking of the building permit was supported by the Council of State. No one had the authority to build their home in the middle of a national park, not even the president.

Erdoğan could have cared less about the legal processes. "Let them tear it down if they can," he said, "They ordered suspension, yet they can't stop the construction of this building. I'll be opening it; I'll be moving in and using it."

In other words: *I will do as I please.*

He further cited the Constitution of the Republic of Turkey, noting that Paragraph 2 of Article 105 reads: "No appeal shall be made to any judicial authority, including the Constitutional Court, against the decisions and orders signed by the President of the Republic on his/her own initiative."[115]

Basically, the president of Turkey is not legally allowed to do whatever he wants, but no one is legally allowed to hold him accountable either outside of impeachment, which in Erdoğan's case is not going to happen.

---

[115] https://en.wikipedia.org/wiki/Presidential_Complex

The Seat in Pergamos

One of the stranger acts of Erdoğan is his determination to rebuild the Temple of Zeus in Pergamos, Turkey. This site has lain in ruins for centuries, but Erdoğan is working to reconstruct it and make it "glorious again" in time for his Vision 2023 program.[116]

In the 19th century, German archaeologists first excavated Pergamos and rediscovered the world-famous Altar of Zeus. They dismantled it and removed it to a museum in Berlin.

In 2013, Erdoğan's government began threatening the German government with various sanctions if they did not return the altar and other artifacts needed to rebuild Zeus' temple.[117]

To the outsider, it seems strange that a strong Muslim leader would be so aggressive regarding the reconstruction of a *pagan* temple, even to the point of returning its idols to it. To those familiar with Islam, however, this doublemindedness is not so strange.

A simpler explanation though is that while Erdoğan is fanatical about Sharia law and the control it gives him over his people, he does not let Sharia law limit himself in any way, shape or form. He does what he pleases.

Erdoğan's stated reason for this reconstruction is to build the largest and best museum of antiquities in the world for the purpose of dramatically increasing Turkey's tourism industry.

Jesus, however, reveals the real reason to us in Revelation.

---

[116] http://shoebat.com/2016/09/01/turkeys-caliph-Erdoğan-is-rebuilding-the-temple-of-zeus-on-a-grand-scale-preparing-it-for-his-2023-grand-vision-for-his-ottoman-caliphate-dream/

[117] http://www.spiegel.de/international/germany/dispute-heats-up-between-germany-and-turkey-over-contested-artifacts-a-888398.html

Two thousand years ago, there was a thriving church in Pergamos. Jesus sent word to the early church in Pergamos saying "I know ... where you dwell, where Satan's throne *is*."[118] Scholarship is in agreement that what Jesus is referring to is the Temple of Zeus in Pergamos, which was considered one of the ancient wonders of the world.[119]

In other words, the Temple of Zeus in Pergamos is considered by Jesus to be the Seat of Satan. So, if Erdoğan is truly the antichrist, then he is the son of Satan, and it would be natural for him to be determined to rebuild his father's throne so he can sit on it.

Interestingly, Adolf Hitler, *an* antichrist, was also fascinated with the Pergamos' altar of Zeus. His architect, Albert Speer, modeled an exact replica of the altar for the construction of the Tribune at Zeppelin Field in Nuremberg. This was the site of major Nazi rallies, and Hitler's podium was placed right in the middle of the altar.

Nazis bowing to Hitler on the altar

---

[118] Revelation 2:13
[119] http://www.visual-arts-cork.com/antiquity/pergamon-altar.htm

Even more curiously, even though the German government publicly refused to return the altar to Erdoğan, the Berlin museum that hosts the original altar closed in February of 2014 in order to "remodel the Pergamon Hall. They said it would not reopen again *for five years* until 2019.[120] *Yet, why in the world would a museum need to close for five years to remodel a wing?* This already sounded suspicious.

A few years later, the museum announced that it was temporarily moving the Pergamon altar to a temporary storage facility during construction. It would not be out of sight during this time and the temporary storage facility would be funded by a "private donor." They also declared the Pergamon Hall would not now reopen for many more years until 2023 because of construction setbacks.[121]

To tie it up in a neat bow, Erdoğan has a master plan for the improvement of Turkey on the world scene called Vision 2023.[122] His stated reason for demanding so forcefully the altar from Germany was to have it set up again and ready for the public in time for the fulfillment of his Vision 2023.

This author believes the Berlin Museum is not just remodeling the Pergamon Hall, but that they are actively (and secretly) transferring the original altar to Turkey for a surprise unveiling in 2023.

He Has Been Named the Supreme Leader of All Muslims

As we explained previously, Islamic prophecy describes an end-times figure called the *mahdi*. The details of who the *mahdi* will be, and what he will do are very similar to the description of the antichrist in Revelation.

---

[120] https://news.artnet.com/art-world/berlins-pergamon-museum-to-close-until-2019-joining-neue-nationalgalerie-in-renovations-1520
[121] http://www.dw.com/en/berlins-pergamon-museum-will-spend-next-eight-years-without-its-famous-altar/a-36337653
[122] https://en.wikipedia.org/wiki/2023_vision

So, it is interesting to note that as we are asking whether Erdoğan could be the antichrist, Muslim scholars around the world have already sent him letters naming him the Supreme Leader of all Muslims. Most importantly, Yusf al-Qaradawi, the president of the International Union of Muslim Scholars, the most influential organization of Muslim scholars in the world, sent Erdoğan a letter after the coup in 2016 saying:

> "Allah is with you and all Arab and Muslim nations are with you including all freedom loving people are with you. We, all the Muslim scholars, in the four corners of the globe, are with you. The Angel Gabriel and the righteous one [in heaven] are with you. And after that the angels will be revealed.
>
> We are all with you. It is because you have stood with righteousness against evil. You are with justice against injustice…
>
> Dear President, lead Turkey as you wish and as we wish … we will be with you giving you strength and will support your party and your loyalists as Allah instructed "O ye who believe fear Allah and stand with the righteous…""

This letter was a strong indication they are ready to declare him the awaited *mahdi*.

Prominent Muslim leaders from around the world are also saying that Erdoğan will declare himself to be the supreme caliph in 2023-2024, and then the Islamic Caliphate will be firmly established.[123] That date, of course, matches Erdoğan's Vision 2023 plan.

---

[123] http://shoebat.com/2017/01/16/major-muslim-leaders-declare-that-within-seven-years-the-muslim-caliphate-will-be-established-and-Erdoğan-will-be-caliph-of-the-muslim-world/

Hater of the Kurds (& Armenians)

Erodgan has an irrational hatred for the Kurdish people.[124]

The Kurds are an ethnic minority people group who live primarily in southwestern Turkey, but also in Northern Syria, Iraq and Iran. Consistently, they have remained a separate people, not mixing with their Arab neighbors for millennia. They have a distinct culture, dietary laws and customs, and even had their own religion (Yazidi) until Muslims forced them to adopt Islam approximately 400 years ago.

Erdoğan has been waging a war against the Kurds for many years[125], and he gets very upset when any of his "allies" like the United States show any political goodwill toward the Kurdish people. He has stated that he considers all Kurds and everyone who supports them to be terrorists.[126]

But why? Why so much hate?

The undisguised hatred is puzzling. The Kurds are a humble and peaceful people. They have never aspired to conquer any state government. They are not sponsors of terrorism as the rest of the world would define it.

For that matter, why do Muslims in Iraq, Iran, and Syria also hate them so much? The only time the Kurds take up arms against anyone is to defend themselves and their rights.

The probable explanation is that the Kurds are likely part of the Lost Tribes of Israel. Over, 2,700 years ago, the Kingdom of Assyria (Turkey) attacked, conquered, and relocated the northern 10 tribes of Israel to the Caucasus mountains. The two tribes who were not conquered, Benjamin, and Judah,

---

[124] https://sputniknews.com/middleeast/201602091034477022-turkey-Erdoğan-kurdophobia-crackdown-kurds/
[125] http://www.nytimes.com/2015/08/31/opinion/turkeys-war-of-distraction-on-kurds.html
[126] http://www.dailystar.com.lb/News/Middle-East/2016/Feb-07/336089-Erdoğan-calls-on-us-to-choose-between-turkey-or-syrian-kurds.ashx

became known collectively as Judah. Most modern-day Jews are descended from them.

Scholars have been searching for the ten Lost Tribes for centuries as there are prophecies predicting the eventual reunion of the northern and southern tribes of Israel. They have successfully identified multiple groups as being highly probable, and the Kurds are candidate number one.

Geographically, they live in exactly the same areas where the Bible says the Lost Tribes were sent. Historically, they have always been an oppressed minority, just as we would expect the lost tribes to be. Culturally, their ancient customs are similar to Jewish customs, even in dietary laws, they observe the Jewish sacred calendar, and their religion is a mixture of Biblical faith with the worship of a bull, just as the Bible says the northern tribes did (wrongly).[127]

Genetics seal the deal. Scientists have determined that the Kurds are the closest genetic relatives to the Jews of anyone else on earth.[128] [129]

So, this explains Erdoğan's irrational hatred very nicely. Satan hates God, but he knows he isn't powerful enough to hurt God, so he does the only thing he can, he tries to hurt God's heart. And the main way to hurt God's heart is to try and destroy God's people that He loves, both Christians and Jews. This explains Hitler, it explains Stalin, it explains a lot of anti-Semitic behavior in history.

It also explains Erdoğan.

Erdoğan also hates the Armenians.[130] [131] No other group receives more vitriol in Turkish media than the Armenians. Erdoğan denies the Armenian

---

[127] http://barcelona.indymedia.org/newswire/display/499718/index.php
[128] http://www.2001translation.com/Kurds.htm
[129] http://dream-prophecy.blogspot.com/2008/08/kurds-and-lost-tribes-of-israel.html
[130] https://en.wikipedia.org/wiki/Anti-Armenian_sentiment
[131] https://pjmedia.com/blog/slogan-in-turkey-during-Erdoğans-rally-armenian-bastards-cannot-deter-us/

genocide.[132] He once said, "They called me a Georgian. Pardon me for saying this, but they said even uglier things: They called me an Armenian!"[133]

As it turns out, Armenians are also considered to be part of the ten Lost Tribes of Israel.[134] DNA research also confirms a strong genetic connection between the Armenians and Israel.[135]

There seems to be a pattern to Erdoğan's hatred.

Conclusions on Erdoğan

So, what are we to conclude? Many dismiss the idea of positively identifying the antichrist simply because they reject the idea of identifying the antichrist at all. They don't believe anyone could do so correctly. Yet, that belief is not biblical.

Throughout Scripture, God has scattered verses about the antichrist specifically so that we could correctly identify him ahead of time and be forewarned. Jesus told us to "watch." God expects us to be watching as we wait, looking for the fulfillment of prophecy.

Just because end-time prophecies have not been fulfilled before, does not mean they cannot be fulfilled now. By definition, they will not be fulfilled until the end times have arrived, not before.

We have spent a lot of time analyzing what the Bible has to say about the coming antichrist, his characteristics, how he'll work, what he'll do; and

---

[132] https://www.theguardian.com/world/2015/apr/15/turkey-cannot-accept-armenia-genocide-label-Erdoğan
[133] https://www.arabnews.com/news/middle-east/612716
[134] http://www.hadassahmagazine.org/2006/02/11/jewish-traveler-armenia/
[135] https://www.jpost.com/Features/Genetics-and-the-Jewish-identity

we've spent a lot of time specifically examining Erdoğan of Turkey to see if he fits the bill.

Here are the things we have confirmed about Erdoğan so far:

- He denies Christ
- He does as he pleases and ignores the laws of his country
- He is looking to change the calendar for Turkey, and if given the chance would do so for the world
- He has changed the laws of Turkey and aspires to see Sharia law adopted everywhere.
- He does not follow the religion of his ancestors as he rejects pagan idols.
- He follows Sufi Islam faithfully and he allows people to give him direct worship
- He has no regard for the "desire of women" in that he rejects the specific idol that refers to.
- He has no regard for the desire of women in that rumors of homosexual relationships with powerful men swirl about him.[136]
- He does seem to worship a "god of forces" as predicted in that he promotes the Ottoman war machine culture (Daniel 11:38).
- He has conquered Turkey and has begun deceptive invasions of Syria, Iraq, and Libya (the 3 "horns").
- He has publicly stated he intends to conquer Syria.
- His name in Greek adds up to 666 as the Apostle John said it would.
- He allows followers to refer to him in divine terms.
- He has built the largest house in the world for himself.
- He is arrogant & boastful.
- He admires and longs to emulate Hitler.
- He is demonstrating an increasing spirit of the antichrist in his persecution of Christians.
- His accomplishments so far fit the description of the early events associated with the *mahdi*.

---

[136] http://shoebat.com/2015/05/23/Erdoğan-the-leader-of-the-antichrist-nation-of-turkey-confirmed-to-be-a-part-of-a-strange-homosexual-cult/

- Has been officially named the leader of all Muslims worldwide by the most influential Muslim scholars, a title belonging to the Caliph, i.e. the *mahdi*.
- Muslim beliefs indicate the *mahdi* is a mirror image of the antichrist in the Bible.
- Christian and Muslim prophecy both seem to indicate the antichrist will rule Turkey.
- Christian and Muslim prophecy both seem to indicate the antichrist will rule Constantinople (Istanbul, former capital of the Roman Empire).
- The antichrist will be Assyrian, and Erdoğan is Turkish (Assyrian).
- He is rebuilding the seat of Satan in Pergamos.
- Erdoğan irrationally hates the Kurds & Armenians, both of whom have been genetically and culturally identified as strong candidates for the Lost Tribes of Israel.

Put all of this together, and the case for Erdoğan being the long-foretold antichrist is strong and compelling. In fact, this author's only hesitation in saying that Erdoğan is definitely the evil one so anticipated is just that we are still in such early stages of prophetic events. More time and a few more events are needed to be sure.

However, if Erdoğan is truly the antichrist, *then that would mean Jesus has already broken the 1st Seal of the Lamb or is in the midst of breaking it.* That would mean the events of Revelation have already begun!

WHAT TO EXPECT NEXT

IF Erdoğan is the antichrist, then what does prophecy tell us he will do next?

As we said before, the most common Western understanding of the antichrist is that of a charismatic leader who is elected to the head of a European Union. He grows in power and hides his evil and even signs a peace treaty with Israel, making the world love him and glorify him. Then, in the middle of this seven-year peace treaty, he reveals his true self, enters the Jewish Temple (reconstructed), stops the sacrifice, and declares himself to be God. From that point forward, he is fully evil and continually wages war on God's people.

Most of that is not correct.

The problem with a lot of the teaching above is that it's generated from conjecture derived from a few biblical verses here and there but does not mesh with the entirety of prophecy well.

Violence

First, as we have said already, there is no biblical requirement for the antichrist to be peaceful or charismatic (though any leader has to have some level of charisma).

In fact, from the antichrist's titles in Scripture to the Book of Revelation saying that from the very beginning he will go out "conquering and to conquer," we should expect him to be violent from the start.

We should expect Erdoğan to be "conquering and to conquer."

So, as Erdoğan has already been conquering, we should see him conquering some new territory.

Exactly How Much Territory Will the Antichrist Control?

Let's review the different passages that describe the arrival of the antichrist:

> *"After this I saw in the night visions, and behold, a fourth beast, dreadful and terrible, exceedingly strong. It had huge iron teeth; it was devouring, breaking in pieces, and trampling the residue with its feet.* **It was different from all the beasts that were before it, and it had ten horns. I was considering the horns, and there was another horn, a little one, coming up among them, before whom three of the first horns were plucked out by the roots**. *And there, in this horn, were eyes like the eyes of a man, and a mouth speaking pompous words...*

> *"Then I wished to know the truth about the fourth beast, which was different from all the others, exceedingly dreadful, with its teeth of iron and its nails of bronze, which devoured, broke in pieces, and trampled the residue with its feet;* **and the ten horns that were on its head, and the other horn which came up, before which three fell,** *namely, that horn which had eyes and a mouth which spoke pompous words, whose appearance was greater than his fellows...*

> *"I was watching; and the same horn was making war against the saints, and prevailing against them, until the Ancient of Days came, and a judgment was made in favor of the saints of the Most High, and the time came for the saints to possess the kingdom.*

"Thus, he said: The fourth beast shall be a fourth kingdom on earth, which shall be different from all other kingdoms, **and shall devour the whole earth, trample it and break it in pieces.** *The ten horns are ten kings who shall arise from this kingdom.* **And another shall rise after them; he shall be different from the first ones and shall subdue three kings.**

"He shall speak pompous words against the Most High, shall persecute the saints of the Most High, and shall intend to change times and law. Then the saints shall be given into his hand for a time and times and half a time.

"But the court shall be seated, and they shall take away his dominion, to consume and destroy it forever. Then the kingdom and dominion, and the greatness of the kingdoms under the whole heaven, shall be given to the people, the saints of the Most High. His kingdom is an everlasting kingdom, and all dominions shall serve and obey Him." (Daniel 7:7-8; 7:19-27)

"Then I stood on the sand of the sea. And I saw a beast rising up out of the sea, having seven heads and ten horns, and on his horns ten crowns, and on his heads a blasphemous name. Now the beast which I saw was like a leopard, his feet were like the feet of a bear, and his mouth like the mouth of a lion. The dragon gave him his power, his throne, and great authority. And I saw one of his heads as if it had been mortally wounded, and his deadly wound was healed. And all the world marveled and followed the beast. So, they worshiped the dragon who gave authority to the beast; and they worshiped the beast, saying, 'Who is like the beast? Who is able to make war with him?'

"And he was given a mouth speaking great things and blasphemies, and he was given authority to continue for

> *forty-two months. Then he opened his mouth in blasphemy against God, to blaspheme His name, His tabernacle, and those who dwell in heaven. It was granted to him to make war with the saints and to overcome them.* ***And authority was given him over every tribe, tongue, and nation.*** *All who dwell on the earth will worship him, whose names have not been written in the Book of Life of the Lamb slain from the foundation of the world."*
> (Revelation 13:1-8)

We have some seemingly contradictory statements here. First, there are numerous places it speaks of the antichrist conquering "three" and ruling over "ten." Having just "ten" crowns.

Yet, there are other verses that say he is given authority "over every tribe, tongue, and nation."

It is possible that the number ten is used in a symbolic sense because ten is a symbol for human government. Therefore, one interpretation could be that the ten horns and ten crowns represent a full governing over the whole earth.

However, the fact it's repeated several times that the antichrist conquers "three," there is no interpretative choice but to see the three as three political divisions, or peoples, or leaders of some kind, which thus indicates the ten are also individual peoples or leaders.

Since the world currently has no global government, and there are not currently ten commonly viewed political divisions, this number does not currently make sense in a global sense (though perhaps at some future date it presumably could).

In light of the ten-nation confederacy described in Psalm 83, we suggest that Scripture is describing the progressive growth of authority of the beast over time.

Logically, anyone who takes power on the earth does so over time. No antichrist will conquer the world in one day. His authority will increase as the beast consumes more and more territory.

We suggest the antichrist will first conquer three peoples/leaders by force. Then, seven more will come under his authority voluntarily, forming the ten-nation confederacy.

This Caliphate will continue to grow and, at some point, will invade Israel. Once it has conquered Jerusalem, it will then grow in its influence and authority, as described in Revelation 13, until it governs most, if not all, of the world.

Let's jump back to our prediction of what Erdoğan will probably do.

First, the Caliphate

If Erdoğan is the antichrist, then he must conquer three nations. As we said before, he has already defeated a coup against himself in Turkey (likely self-engineered), effectively conquering his own country. He's already moved tanks and troops into Syria, Iraq, and Libya.

We should see in the coming years Erdoğan finish the conquest of Syria, Iraq and Libya (or maybe another). Those would complete the three horns he is to conquer. Since there is no mention of Aram (Syria) or Damascus (Syria) or Babylon (Iraq) in the list of nations found in Psalm 83, but Assyria is indicated as the leader, it matches that modern Syria and Iraq would be controlled by modern Turkey (Assyria).

Once the third horn has fallen, the confederacy must be announced. After all, if the other seven countries want to align themselves with the antichrist, there must be some official alliance or confederacy they can join.

Therefore, Erdoğan's next step would likely be an official announcement of an Islamic Caliphate with him at its head as the Caliph.

In 2018, Erdoğan called a summit of all the Islamic nations of the World to review their ties to "terrorist Israel," in response to the United States opening its new embassy in Jerusalem.[137]

Cleary, Erdoğan views himself as the leader of the Islamic World who will unite them with one voice against Israel. What's missing is the other leaders' willingness to relinquish their individual authority and submit to his.

While we are hearing the voices of many *religious* Muslim leaders calling for the recognition of Erdoğan as the Caliph, Muslim *political* leaders of other nations do not yet seem ready.

However, while Turkey is currently the 13th largest economy in the world, if Erdoğan were to add Syria and Iraq to his belt, his new Caliphate would jump up to 9th place in the world economy, *pushing the United Kingdom down to 10th and France down to 11th.*

This is his stated goal for his Vision 2023 plan, to be in the top ten world economies by 2023. So, we should definitely look for him to make that move in the next few years.

We can easily imagine a dramatic shift in Middle Eastern politics at that juncture.

There is an economic organization called the Gulf Cooperation Council, an alliance of six nations: Bahrain, Kuwait, Oman, Qatar, Saudi Arabia, and the United Arab Emirates. These nations are the wealthiest Sunni Muslim nations, they are the most likely to ally themselves with Erdoğan, and they are the same peoples identified by the prophet who wrote Psalm 83 as forming the confederacy.

If they were to join Erdoğan voluntarily at that point, *the Islamic Caliphate would then have a combined GDP of $6.5 Trillion,* rocketing it up past Germany, past Japan, and into 4th place in the world right behind India and

---

[137] http://www.breitbart.com/jerusalem/2018/05/15/turkey-calls-summit-urges-islamic-world-to-review-ties-to-terror-state-israel/

the United States. (It should be noted that the addition of these 6 countries to Turkey, Syria, Iraq, and Libya would be a total of 10 nations, i.e. "ten horns.")

The combined populations would make them the 6th or 7th most populous nation in the world and would launch them to 4th place in terms of global military spending, close to passing both China and the European Union. With a little effort, their military would be second only to the United States.

At such a moment, Erdoğan would definitely make the call for those Sunni nations to join him. To join for economic glory, for prestige in the world, for the dignity of Muslims everywhere, for the glory of Islam, and for the punishment of Israel.

Muslim scholars and imams across the globe would be calling for the same. It is no stretch to think these Sunni leaders might be compelled to agree.

If Libya or Azerbaijan is not included in the original Caliphate, then the seventh to join could be Jordan, Israel's western neighbor. They are already in talks to join the Gulf Cooperation Council, and they would complete the peoples described in Psalm 83.

That also would make ten.

The War with Israel

On May 15th, 2018, Erdoğan said of Benjamin Netanyahu, Prime Minister of Israel, "Netanyahu is the PM of an apartheid state that has occupied a defenseless people's lands for [sixty years plus] in violation of UN resolutions. He has the blood of Palestinians on his hands..." [138]

He also ejected the Israeli ambassador from Turkey and called for a world summit of Islamic nations to discuss responding to Israel more forcefully.

---

[138] https://www.israelnationalnews.com/News/News.aspx/246031

What event provoked such actions? Dozens of Palestinians were killed on the day the United States historically opened its embassy in Jerusalem. Turkey would like to maintain this was a massacre of innocents by an oppressor, Israel.

Yet, those Gaza Palestinians who were killed were participating in riots at the Israeli border. The rioters were organized and paid by the terrorist organization Hamas to be there.[139] They were trying to illegally infiltrate Israel *en masse*.

Israel has a policy of only shooting men that are observed to be holding or throwing an explosive device or weapon that poses an immediate threat. Hamas runs the Gaza Strip and has been globally recognized as a radical terrorist organization for decades. They regularly launch explosive missiles at innocent Israeli neighborhoods across the border just for kicks.

Given that tens of thousands of Palestinians rioted at the border that day and tried to break down the fence – and that many of them were holding weapons – it is a miracle only several dozen were killed. Frankly, every single one of those killings was quite justified.

Historically, whenever Hamas agents have successfully broken into Israel, they immediately head for residential neighborhoods and slit the throats of innocents.[140] Unfortunately, these acts of terror are being encouraged and called for by top Palestinian government officials.[141] In June of 2016, a top aide to Palestinian president Mahmoud Abbas said in a public statement, "Wherever you find an Israeli, slit his throat."

---

[139] https://www.algemeiner.com/2018/05/15/hamas-paying-protesters-to-charge-gaza-border-israel-reveals/
[140] http://www1.cbn.com/cbnnews/israel/2016/july/netanyahu-on-teens-murder-you-dont-slit-a-little-girls-throat-for-peace
[141] http://www.timesofisrael.com/abbas-aide-wherever-you-see-an-israeli-slit-his-throat/?fb_comment_id=1004784799642815_1004863149634980#f3c859d6b398fbc

Doesn't the Turkish government know these facts? Of course, it does. *Turkey is actually the one supplying cash to Hamas so Hamas can pay civilians to storm the border.*[142]

That means Erdoğan is the one funding the massacres, leaving Israel with no choice but to respond, but then has the gall to lie about it and condemn Israel for responding when he himself left them no choice.

Erdoğan is not only the father of the Islamic State, but he is now the father of Hamas. He is using the same methodology. As Scripture says, "he will cause deceit to prosper."

Of Hamas, he said to Netanyahu, "Hamas is not a terrorist organization and Palestinians are not terrorists."[143] Erdoğan is both lawless and shameless.

Netanyahu rightfully responded, "A man whose hands are stained with the blood of countless Kurdish citizens in Turkey and Syria is the last one who can preach to us about combat ethics."

One important point to note here is that while technically the Gazans are Philistines by ethnicity, the collective Palestinian people which includes millions in the West Bank would be identified as Jordanians, i.e. the Children of Lot.

Psalm 83 says that the Assyrian (antichrist) leads the confederacy of Muslim nations against Israel in order "to help the Children of Lot." *At this point, it is no stretch at all to imagine Erdoğan raising a coalition of Muslims nations to attack Israel for perceived or staged oppressions of the Palestinian people.*

No stretch at all.

This particular event will not be the event that launches the war. It was not big enough. No, something else much bigger will provoke it. This author

---

[142] https://ahvalnews.com/israel-turkey/turkish-funding-hamas-military-exposed-arrest-report
[143] https://www.israelnationalnews.com/News/News.aspx/246031

believes that it will not happen until *after* the declaration of the Caliphate by Erdoğan in 2023, but probably not much after.

Note: Much of this section of this book is speculation, but we believe it is educated speculation. At this time, the best theory seems to be that Erdoğan will finish conquering Syria and Iraq before 2023, announce the Islamic Caliphate in 2023, and then raise a coalition of nations to attack Israel soon after that.

The Tribulation

THE TRIBULATION IS a seven-year period filled with terrible events troubling the earth right before Jesus Christ returns at the Second Coming.

Many prophecy books say the beginning of this period is marked by the Revealing of the Antichrist. They also suppose he will control of the whole world the entire seven years, but neither is a good supposition based on Scripture.

Scripture does indeed lay out a seven-year period of great Tribulation upon the earth. Muslim prophecy also describes a seven-year rule by the *mahdi* at the end of the world.

However, as already explained, the Bible really teaches the antichrist will be revealed long before the Tribulation begins (and we believe he already has been revealed). The beginning of the Tribulation is not marked by the arrival of the antichrist, but by the appearance of the Two Witnesses in Jerusalem.

Also, a close examination of Revelation shows the antichrist will probably not be in full control over much of the earth until the *second* half of the Tribulation. By definition, conquest takes time.

So, what exactly is the Tribulation?

The word Tribulation means "trouble" or "affliction." It is rooted in the word for an ancient wooden-handled tool, a *tribulum,* that had sharp iron teeth and was used for threshing grain. To thresh grain is to beat it and crush it for the purpose of separating the edible part of the grain from the inedible part, the chaff.

John the Baptist said of Jesus:

> *"I indeed baptize you with water unto repentance, but He who is coming after me is mightier than I, whose sandals I am not worthy to carry. He will baptize you with the Holy Spirit and fire. His winnowing fan is in His hand, and He will thoroughly clean out His threshing floor, and gather His wheat into the barn; but He will burn up the chaff with unquenchable fire."*
> (Matthew 3:11-12)

From the wheat's perspective, threshing is a brutal process. From the thresher's perspective, threshing is a brutal process that is done for a good purpose, to separate the worthless from the valuable. Yet, He knows the brutal process must be engaged for that which is valuable to become useful.

From the Bible's perspective, God is the One doing the threshing. He threshes the world to separate the believers from the unbelievers, and to strengthen and purify the believers.

So, the Tribulation is the Great Threshing of the world. God is constantly threshing the world of course, as He has for thousands of years, but there is coming a time of Great Threshing, a time when the entire world is threshed at the same time and at a level greater than ever before. When this process is complete, the harvest will be complete.

Now, the Bible is not European-centric, nor is it American-centric. It's not even global-centric. The Bible is always Middle Eastern-centric, specifically *Israel*-centric.

That means that when the Bible is referring to a Great Threshing, a Tribulation, it can only be referring to a time of great trouble for Israel specifically.

That does not mean that there are not judgments happening in the rest of the world during that time. It means that the rest of the world could begin experiencing tribulations and problems long before the 7-year period begins, but that for *Israel*, the period of trial will be limited to 7 years.

The Bible says that there are exactly 3.5 years between the beginning of the Tribulation and the moment when the antichrist kills the Two Witnesses and enters the Temple, declaring himself to be God.

In a world of increasing wars, earthquakes, pestilences and other troubles, how do you then mark the exact moment the Tribulation begins?

If there is an exact time measurement, there *has* to be a marking moment, an event that starts the clock ticking and is a big enough moment the whole world could recognize it as the moment the Tribulation began.

We've already said the Two Witnesses preach for those same 3.5 years, so their arrival marks the beginning of the Tribulation. But why do they show up? What event causes them to begin their preaching ministry – a ministry that is apparently offensive enough that people (and possibly even the Israeli government itself) try to stop them, only to be supernaturally stopped themselves by God's power.

> *"And I will appoint my Two Witnesses, and they will prophesy for 1,260 days [3.5 years], clothed in sackcloth. They are 'the two olive trees' and the two lampstands, and 'they stand before the Lord of the earth.'* ***If anyone tries to harm them, fire comes from their mouths and devours their enemies.*** *This is how anyone who wants to harm them must die.* ***They have power to shut up the heavens so that it will not rain during the time they are prophesying; and they have power to turn the waters into blood and to strike the earth with every kind of plague as often as they want.***
>
> *"Now when they have finished their testimony, the beast that comes up from the Abyss will attack them, and overpower and kill them. Their bodies will lie in the public square of the great city—which is figuratively called*

"Sodom and Egypt—where also their Lord was crucified. For three and a half days some from every people, tribe, language and nation will gaze on their bodies and refuse them burial. The inhabitants of the earth will gloat over them and will celebrate by sending each other gifts, because these two prophets had tormented those who live on the earth."

"But after the three and a half days the breath of life from God entered them, and they stood on their feet, and terror struck those who saw them. Then they heard a loud voice from heaven saying to them, "Come up here." And they went up to heaven in a cloud, while their enemies looked on." (Revelation 11:3-12)

The Two Witnesses arrive on the scene for a *reason*. Their message will likely be a strong call to repentance combined with encouragement of God's willingness to forgive, and a prediction of the temporary victory of the antichrist while simultaneously condemning him as being evil incarnate.

The reasons they begin to preach *when* they do could be a threatened invasion by the antichrist, or an actual invasion of the antichrist. Which it is, we don't know for sure, but Scripture is clear that their ministry ends with the antichrist successfully entering Jerusalem and killing them.

Regardless, what Revelation 11 makes clear is that at some point during the time of the Two Witnesses (3.5 years), the antichrist will invade Israel.

The Invasion

When that happens, Israel, of course, will not just roll over. By law, every single citizen is required to join the Israeli military when they come of age, both men and women. Their tactics and strategic thinking are incredible, superior to all other militaries. Their weaponry is highly sophisticated, well-funded, and extremely effective.[144]

In fact, global studies repeatedly show Israel as among the top militaries in the world. Currently, their armed forces are ranked strongest in the Middle East, while their air force is considered the best in the world.[145]

Lastly, their determination is born of self-survival among a sea of enemies. No, Israel will not roll over easily. They will not give up. History has taught them well just how high the stakes are.

In spite of the probable financial and military strength of an Islamic Caliphate, the Caliphate's determination to win will be born of lust for conquest and hatred, things that can never motivate as strongly as the need to survive that drives Israel. Also, while the Caliphate's weaponry, tactics, and organization will be good, it will still be light years behind Israel's.

So, Erdoğan will not take Israel in a day, not even with a battle raging on two fronts if Egypt attacks from the south. It would likely take him months, and even the full 3.5 years does not seem outside the realm of possibility.

In fact, the only way Erdoğan could have success at all would be because of access to significantly more resources. Even then, there would also have to be an apathetic, absent, or even destroyed United States (more on those possibilities later).

The Two Witnesses

We've mentioned the Two Witnesses several times already, but who exactly are they?

---

[144] https://www.haaretz.com/who-has-the-mideast-s-strongest-military-1.5321268
[145] https://www.jpost.com/Israel-News/Israels-air-force-the-best-in-the-world-study-finds-380030

They are two mysterious men of God who begin preaching during the Tribulation. Revelation 11:3 says they will prophesy (preach) for 1,260 days, which equals 3.5 years. Later, Revelation says that the Beast (antichrist) kills them after completing those 3.5 years, enters the Temple, and then proceeds to persecute God's people for another 3.5 years for a total of 7 years before Jesus returns.

This is why we know the 7-year Tribulation begins with the launch of Two Witness' ministry. That is the only way the math works.

The Two Witnesses are not the cause of Israel's Tribulation, but a response to it. We believe that the best guess (note that we do not say this absolutely) is that the Caliphate under Erdoğan will initiate military hostilities (bombings, ground invasion, or some other form) and the Two Witnesses will begin preaching in Jerusalem the same day.

They will likely prophesy that Israelis need to repent of their sins and accept *Yeshua* (Jesus) as their Messiah because the Caliphate is going to win and conquer Israel. Obviously, this message, while true, would *not* be very popular with the people and especially the Israeli government.

The Israeli government would almost certainly consider their public preaching to be an act of treason, especially if accompanied by miracles of any kind validating their words. Without a doubt, the Israeli government would send squads of soldiers to remove them forcibly.

That is why the passage says *"And if anyone wants to harm them, fire proceeds from their mouth and devours their enemies. And if anyone wants to harm them, he must be killed in this manner."*

This is reminiscent of Elijah when he called down fire from heaven to devour numerous squadrons of soldiers who'd been sent by an evil king of Israel to arrest him.

In fact, many scholars believe that the Two Witnesses are actually Elijah and Moses themselves returned to earth for this special mission.

Why?

1) They not only have the power to burn up attackers with fire, but they can cause rain to be withheld from the earth, they can turn water to blood, and they can strike the earth with plagues. The first two are miracles that Elijah was able to do, the last two are what Moses did.

2) Both Elijah and Moses were supernaturally re-moved from the earth by God. Elijah was taken to Heaven in a whirlwind (never died) and Moses' body was hidden away by God. Besides Enoch who lived before Noah's flood, these are the only two men who were taken up in this way.

3) Elijah is the chief of the Prophets, and Moses is the giver of the Law. Therefore, if the real identity of the Two Witnesses proves to be Moses and Elijah, then Israel will literally experience a witness/judgment from the Law and the Prophets (a term often used to mean the Old Testament).

The Breech of Jerusalem

"When they finish their testimony, the beast that ascends out of the bottomless pit will make war against them, overcome them, and kill them. And their dead bodies will lie in the street of the great city which spiritually is called Sodom and Egypt where also our Lord was crucified. Then those from the peoples, tribes, tongues, and nations will see their dead bodies three-and-a-half days, and not allow their dead bodies to be put into graves. And those who

dwell on the earth will rejoice over them, make merry, and send gifts to one another, because these two prophets tormented those who dwell on the earth.

"Now after the three-and-a-half days the breath of life from God entered them, and they stood on their feet, and great fear fell on those who saw them. And they heard a loud voice from heaven saying to them, "Come up here." And they ascended to heaven in a cloud, and their enemies saw them. In the same hour there was a great earthquake, and a tenth of the city fell. In the earthquake seven thousand people were killed, and the rest were afraid and gave glory to the God of heaven."
(Revelation 11:7-13)

So, after the Two Witnesses have preached for the 3.5 years, the Beast (Caliphate) finally overcomes them and kills them. Other prophecies say that at this point in time, the antichrist also enters the Temple, stops the sacrifices, and declares himself to be God.

This means that the day the Two Witnesses fall is the same day Jerusalem falls. For the next 3.5 years, Israel will be completely ruled by the antichrist and God's people will constantly flee persecution.

The verses cited above emphasize that the Two Witnesses caused plagues and droughts to affect many peoples around the world, not just locally. When the antichrist kills them, the world celebrates like it's Christmas, even giving gifts to each other. It is clear at this point the majority of the world is under the influence of the enemy.

This second half of the Tribulation is referred to by theologians as the Great Tribulation because the persecution intensifies so dramatically.

The Expansion

This is the halfway point. This is when the antichrist requires his mark on everyone's hand or forehead and declares that no one can buy or sell without it.

It is at this time when the antichrist seems to expand his territory:

> *"Now the beast which I saw was like a leopard, his feet were like the feet of a bear, and his mouth like the mouth of a lion. The dragon gave him his power, his throne, and great authority" (Revelation 13:2)*

From the Book of Daniel, we know what these animals represent. The leopard is a symbol for Greece (originally under Alexander the Great), the bear is Persia (Iran), and the Lion represents Assyria and/or Babylon (Iraq).

This verse is given to us *after* the death of the Two Witnesses and the conquest of Israel in Revelation 11. The Beast (Caliphate) already existed, but now in Chapter 13, it grows in territory.

The best interpretation of this is that the Caliphate expands soon after conquering Israel to include the entire Middle East, Iran, probably North Africa, and even Greece and the Muslim peoples of Eastern Europe.

Later in Chapter 13, it says *"It was granted to him to make war with the saints and to overcome them. And authority was given him over every tribe, tongue, and nation."*

So, the Caliphate then either expands to cover the entire world, or at least exerts authority over the entire world in the same way that the United States has held authority over the world in recent generations. Which it will be is unclear, though this author would lean toward the latter.

One reason being that there is another entity, the Whore of Babylon (Revelation 17) who *rides* the Beast, meaning she is distinct from the Beast, not synonymous with the Beast. This is confirmed absolutely in Revelation 18 when the Beast eats the Whore. (The Whore is probably Europe, but more on this later.)

Also, if the United States, Russia, and China have all been severely weakened by devastating wars, an Islamic Caliphate would have a much easier time dominating the world.

The Four Horsemen

> "Now I saw when the Lamb opened one of the seals; and I heard one of the four living creatures saying with a voice like thunder, 'Come and see.' And I looked, and behold, a white horse. He who sat on it had a bow; and a crown was given to him, and he went out conquering and to conquer." (Revelation 6:1-2)

If Erdoğan is indeed the antichrist, then Jesus has already begun breaking the 1st seal, or maybe even fully broken it.

> "When He opened the second seal, I heard the second living creature saying, 'Come and see.' Another horse, fiery red, went out. And it was granted to the one who sat on it to take peace from the earth, and that people should kill one another; and there was given to him a great sword." (Revelation 6:3-4)

If the 1st seal is already broken, then the next event to occur would be Jesus' breaking the 2nd seal. Remember that the breaking of each seal is a step towards Jesus taking possession of His Kingdom.

When He breaks the 2nd seal, the red horse rides. And the red horse stands for war.

> "When He opened the third seal, I heard the third living creature say, 'Come and see.' So I looked, and behold, a black horse, and he who sat on it had a pair of scales in his hand. And I heard a voice in the midst of the four living creatures saying, "A quart of wheat for a denarius, and three quarts of barley for a denarius; and do not harm the oil and the wine."

> "When He opened the fourth seal, I heard the voice of the fourth living creature saying, 'Come and see.' So I looked,

and behold, a pale horse. And the name of him who sat on it was Death, and Hades followed with him. And power was given to them over a fourth of the earth, to kill with sword, with hunger, with death, and by the beasts of the earth." (Revelation 6:5-8)

Breaking the 3rd and 4th seals brings the black and sickly green horses who represent economic devastation (and famine) and plague respectively. Many prophecy commentators have interpreted these devastations as being successive on top of each other in the same geographic area.

They believe the antichrist will appear and conquer lands which naturally leads to a great war. The war then brings economic devastation and famine, and then all those dead bodies combined with poor sanitation and severe malnutrition creates a terrible outbreak of disease.

Yet, let's pay special attention to verse 8. It says, *"And power was given to them [each horseman] over a fourth of the earth, to kill with sword, with hunger, with death, and by the beasts of the earth."*

There are two ways to read that verse. Either all four horses are given power over the *same* 25% of the earth, or each horse is given a *different* 25% of the earth.

Note that both interpretations limit the antichrist's influence (conquest) to 25% of the earth's territory at this point. This is further proof he does not achieve global influence until Revelation 13.

In the first option, where each devastation leads to the next within the same geographic area, 75% of the global population would remain unaffected by the breaking of the seals.

Does that seem likely? Probably not.

Thankfully, another place in Scripture references these same horses and gives us more info (though for some reason the passage is often overlooked). The prophet Zechariah says:

> *"Then I turned and raised my eyes and looked, and behold, four chariots were coming from between two mountains, and the mountains were mountains of bronze. With the first chariot were red horses, with the second chariot black horses, with the third chariot white horses, and with the fourth chariot dappled horses—strong steeds."*
> *(Zechariah 6:1-3)*

Zechariah, like Revelation and Daniel, is a book with a lot of space dedicated to end-times prophecy. Of immediate notice is that these are the same exact four colors of the horsemen given in Revelation 6.

Next, and most importantly, Zechariah tells us *where* the horses go:

> *"'The one with the black horses is going to the north country, the white are going after them, and the dappled are going toward the south country.' Then the strong steeds went out, eager to go, that they might walk to and fro throughout the earth."*
> *(Zechariah 6:6-7a)*

This is an interesting viewpoint of the horses/horsemen. Zechariah gives us clear compass directions as guidance for which catastrophe will strike which part of the earth. Strangely, though, the black horse and the white horse are given in a different order than in Revelation, and the direction of the red horses is not mentioned at all.

The answer to this mystery is in remembering that the Bible is Israel-centric. Revelation is describing the arrival of the horses chronologically, i.e. in what order they first affect the earth anywhere. On the other hand, Zechariah has a geographical focus. In his vision, the horses appear almost simultaneously.

Zechariah's focus is to explain their movements after they appear.

Since Zechariah's viewpoint is from Israel, we must first imagine what he is seeing geographically. He is seeing two bronze colored mountains, and the four chariots come from between those mountains. In what direction from Zechariah's position would the mountains be?

To his west lies the Mediterranean Ocean, so the mountains would not be to the west of him. Since some of the horses go north from the mountains, and some of the horses go south, the mountains themselves can only be to the east of him. In his vision, they are to the east, and the horses ride out from there to the north and to the south, but not to the west because of the ocean.

We have speculated so far that the antichrist starts in Assyria and rules the Middle East surrounding Israel, but that the Caliphate "eats" Europe some time *after* the conquest of Israel.

If we match the black horse of Revelation (famine, economic devastation) to the black horse of Zechariah (the north), then we can predict that when Jesus breaks the 3rd seal, economic devastation and/or possibly famine will strike the north, i.e. Europe.

If we marry that understanding to Revelation 18 where the Beast devours the Whore (Europe), then Zechariah's perspective makes perfect sense. From his perspective in Israel, the white horse (antichrist) remains in the Middle East for a time, but later follows the black horse to Europe.

The 4th horse in Revelation is called the Pale Horse, but the Greek word is *chloros*, which is translated as a sickly green, or ash-colored, meaning the color of a sick person's face. The 4th horse in Zechariah is described with the Hebrew *barod*, which is best translated as white speckles on grey, i.e. ash-colored. These are the same horse.

When Jesus breaks the 4th seal, plague erupts. It would seem Zechariah is telling us the plague strikes Africa in the south.

Which then leaves the red horses. Where do they go? Why is a direction not given?

Well, if they don't go in a direction, logically that means that they stay where they are. Therefore, if the mountains are in the east, then the red horses are in the east as well.

According to Revelation 6, when Jesus breaks the 2nd seal, war breaks out. If our interpretation of Zechariah is correct, then war will break out among the Asian countries. These wars could include India and Pakistan, but they will most *certainly* involve China and the Koreas, the Philippines, and Japan.

It is impossible to imagine a war involving China and our allies like the Philippines, Japan, and South Korea that would not by necessity draw the United States into it. This would be a global Pacific-centric war, which would take place to the "east" of Israel.

Another valid interpretation of Zechariah 6:7 is *"Then the strong [colored] steeds went out, eager to go, that they might walk to and fro throughout the [ends of the] earth."*

It is possible to interpret the Hebrew word for "strong" there as referring to the bold color of the red horses, like blood.

Even if this interpretation is correct, however, the result is the same. The red horses go to the ends of the earth, i.e. War goes to the far east and the far west: United States and China.

The 2nd Seal

WAR

WE'VE SEEN THE establishment of the Islamic Caliphate, led by Turkey, could create, almost overnight, a brand new superpower based in the Middle East. This Caliphate would be extremely strategic geographically and in control of much of the world's oil. They would be a major player instantly.

However, any effort by the Caliphate to exert power over Israel would be hampered by the strong presence of the United States as Israel's best and most determined ally.

Honestly, no Middle Eastern power, not even a superpower like the Caliphate, could successfully pressure Israel in the current political environment. Not even if Europe became wholly submissive to the Caliphate (and the E.U. already is somewhat submissive to Erdoğan). The United States still leads Europe and the rest of the world, not the other way around.

So, something drastic would have to change. There are only three real possible shifts that could alter the environment enough to allow the Caliphate free reign with Israel:

1.) The United States is angered and breaks its friendship with Israel.
2.) The United States is distracted by other events and so it cannot help Israel.
3.) The United States is weakened and so it cannot help Israel.

Angered, distracted, or weakened.

A change in the presidency could indeed bring about the first option. We already saw this under Barack Obama who actively worked to undermine

Israel on the world scene and used our intelligence agencies to help Erdoğan take the first steps to establish the Caliphate.

Still, we have Revelation saying that there will be war. A great war that impacts 25% of the world. War in the east, and the ends of the earth. Most certainly involving China as there can be no significant war in the Far East that would not involve China.

China is currently threatening war against Japan, South Korea, Taiwan, Australia, the Philippines, and India – all of whom are our allies. If war broke out between these Asian nations, *and even if the United States were not somehow drawn in*, at a minimum supply lines and the Pacific shipping industry would be enormously disrupted.

Trade between the United States and China is so interwoven that such a disruption would put the United States in a position where we suddenly would not be able to manufacture many things: from paper products to cars and computers, even military equipment and aircraft.

Furthermore, China currently holds enormous amounts of U.S. Treasury bonds and has huge levels of other kinds of investments in many American industries and real estate. If hostilities broke out, they could take economic actions against the United States and its currency.

A global Pacific War would immediately and severely weaken the United States. We could overcome these obstacles of course, and reactivate much of our manufacturing sector, but those efforts would take time. At least several years.

And during that time, if we find ourselves facing a severe shortage of materials needed to manufacture armaments and military equipment, the United States would be in no position to come to anybody's aid, not even Israel's.

Of course, if the United States is actually drawn into a global war with China, we would be both distracted and weakened, and even less able to help Israel against a third superpower, the Caliphate.

Isaiah 18

ISAIAH 18 IS considered by many scholars to be the most difficult chapter in the entire Bible to interpret. It can be found in the middle of a bunch of end-of-the-world prophecies predicting the future of many Muslim nations, including Iraq, Jordan, Syria, Lebanon, and Egypt.

Your Bible may have a header that reads something like "Message to Ethiopia" or "Prophecy Against Ethiopia." The reason for this is a reference in the first verses to "Cush," an ancient name for Ethiopia or Sudan. (Cush is a Hebrew word literally meaning "black" or "black people.")

However, the reference Isaiah 18 does not actually identify the nation receiving the prophecy as being Cush itself, but as being a country that "lies beyond the waters of Cush."

Scholars freely admit it is unknown exactly which nation Isaiah refers to in Chapter 18 (though the other peoples of Chapters 14 – 24 are identifiable).

Isaiah himself doesn't seem to know which nation his prophecy refers to.

Isaiah doesn't know its name but calls it the "land shadowed with buzzing wings" and the "land that lies beyond the waters of the black people." Verse 7 implies that he doesn't recognize the language they speak either, though presumably he would have recognized the languages of any neighboring countries, just as today we would recognize when someone was speaking Spanish, French, German, Italian, or Japanese.

The reason we know Chapters 14 – 27 are prophecies regarding the end times is most of the prophecies detailed there have not yet been fulfilled.[146] They describe the final destructions of several of Israel's neighbors.

---

[146] Specifically, Chapters 14 – 19 appear to be end-times prophecies, as well as 24 – 27. Chapters 20 – 23 had fulfillments in Isaiah's lifetime, but contain some portions that had a double future meaning, similar to Isaiah 9, "For unto us a Child is born…"

Some Say It's the United States

Some scholars have suggested that the nation of Isaiah 18 could be the United States. The reason the Isaiah 18 nation has been so difficult to definitively identify is the same reason it is hard to absolutely conclude it *is* speaking of America: Many of the Hebrew words in this chapter have multiple possible interpretations.

In other words, there are many possible translations of this Hebrew passage, though we believe that only one truly makes sense.

Here is what we know for sure:

1.) The Isaiah 18 nation must exist during the end times.
2.) It must be of some significance during the end times in relation to Israel and global events.
3.) Isaiah didn't recognize the people and considered their appearance strange. He also seemed to not recognize their language.

Following is one of the standard translations of the first part of Isaiah 18:

"Woe to the land shadowed with buzzing wings,
Which is beyond the rivers of Ethiopia,
Which sends ambassadors by sea,
Even in vessels of reed on the waters, saying,
'Go, swift messengers, to a nation tall and smooth of skin,
To a people terrible from their beginning onward,
A nation powerful and treading down,
Whose land the rivers divide.'"
(Isaiah 18:1-2, NKJV)

Because scholars aren't sure which nation is being described, *they don't have any context to help them when choosing between multiple possible translations of various Hebrew words.* And as we shall see, that lack of context has caused them often to choose inappropriate translations in several places in order to "force a fit."

Verse 1 reads *"Which is beyond the rivers of Ethiopia."* Yet, we've already seen Ethiopia is a bad translation as the political boundaries that make up Ethiopia today didn't exist three thousand years ago. The Hebrew word is *Cush*, which literally means "black" or "black people."

This could refer to Ethiopia and/or Sudan (historically referred to as Cush), or it could be referring to black populations in general, meaning all of Sub-Saharan Africa. Since either is possible, we should not rule either out, but let the rest of the passage guide us.

Second, this nation absolutely *cannot* be Cush itself, but must be a *different* mysterious country that lies *beyond* Cush.

What does Isaiah mean by "beyond"? From Israel, beyond can only mean further south or further west. So, we should be looking for a country that fits the rest of the description yet is located to the south or the west of Sudan and Ethiopia.

Verse 2 says, *"Which sends envoys by sea in papyrus boats over the water. Go, swift messengers, to a people tall and smooth-skinned, to a people feared far and wide, an aggressive nation of strange speech, whose land is divided by rivers."* (NIV)

There are several distinctive identifiers here that help us:

A.) It is a nation known for sending people out with messages (Hebrew: **ṣî·rîm** – envoys, ambassadors, messengers).

B.) This nation sends out these messengers over the waters. (Hebrew: **ma·yim** - not rivers, but waters – They are connected to large bodies of waters, i.e. oceans).

C.) The people of this country are unusually tall in Isaiah's mind, at least as compared to Israelites of his day (Hebrew: **mashak** – drawn out, stretched out, meaning "tall").

D.) The people are said to be "smooth-skinned" (Hebrew: **marat** – literally peeled, or to be made bald, i.e. to remove the hair.) So, these people are not naturally smooth-skinned, but shave their beards and/or other body hair.

The NIV says these people are "feared far and wide," but other translations say "To a people terrible from their beginning onward" (NKJV).

The Hebrew word for terrible (**nōwrā**) actually means "awesome" or "fearsome." This is a militarily fearsome people from the beginning. (The "far and wide" translation is a bad translation. The Hebrew literally means "from the beginning and until now.")

The Hebrew word for aggressive is **qavqav**. Honestly, the exact meaning of this word is unknown today, but only because this is the only place in the Old Testament that specific form of it is used. The root of this word is *qavah*, which means "strong," originally deriving from the idea of the strength of a firm, taut, corded rope.

So, if *qavah* means firm strength, then *qavqav* is a repetition of *qavah* twice for emphasis. Hebrew does this a lot. When a word is to be emphasized, it is repeated. For example, In Genesis 2:17, God said to Adam, "but of the tree of the knowledge of good and evil you shall not eat, for in the day that you eat of it you shall surely die." Yet, the actual Hebrew does not say "you shall surely die," rather it says, "you will die die" or "you will die dying."

The repetition is for emphasis. So, rather than describing this people as "aggressive," Isaiah is actually saying they are either "super strong" or "extremely firm." A better translation would seem to be "very firmly resolved" (They are strong because of firm unity like a corded rope).

We also see that this country's land is divided by a river(s) (end of verse 2).

Now, let's survey all the possible fits across time and space. Starting with Isaiah's time (roughly 750 BC) and scanning the annals and records of history through modern day, are there now or has there ever been any militarily fearsome country on the African continent whose territory is divided by a river?

None come to mind? That's because there have not been any militarily fearsome nations on the African continent. Not in Isaiah's time, and not today. Especially none whose land is divided by a river.

The *only* country in Africa that could come close would be Egypt because at one time they had a powerful military and their land is divided by the Nile. *However,* they do not lie on the *other side of* Cush (beyond), but on the same side as Israel. Plus, by Isaiah's time Egypt was much weaker and had suffered many military defeats. (Also, Isaiah 19 is about Egypt, so Chapter 18 must be about a different people.)

And we've already established these chapters of Isaiah are dealing with end times prophecies and we've also established that we are very likely now living in the end times. We need to look at Africa today and ask if there are *currently* any militarily strong countries feared from their beginning.

Again, the answer is no.

It Seems to Fit

Therefore, if we limit the meaning of Cush to being the geographical territory controlled by Ethiopia or Sudan today, then Isaiah 18 has no meaning because there are no possible candidates, *nor can there ever be as any corresponding nation has to have been fearsome from its beginning.* African nations all have long histories already and so all are disqualified from consideration.

On the other hand, if we allow the Hebrew to breathe and don't force it into such a narrow box, a very reasonable translation is:

> *"Woe to the land…that lies on the other side of the waters of the black race."*

With such an understanding, now it becomes possible to look at other candidates. Nations that lie on the other side of the Atlantic Ocean.

So, how many countries in the Americas have been militarily fearsome since their beginning, and are divided by a river(s)? Only one: The United States.

In fact, besides the United States, are there *any* counties anywhere in the world that have been militarily fearsome since their beginning and still are today?

No, again, only America. And this is because it is a very young country compared to the rest of the world. The United States has not yet had a decline of its national strength like China or Persia or Rome.

To be perfectly honest, America is the only possibility, yet does the rest of Isaiah 18 fit?

Our land is indeed divided in half by a system of major rivers in the middle of our country that feed the central Mississippi.

What about the messengers/ambassadors? Sure, the United States like many countries sends ambassadors all over the world, though the U.S. is arguably more involved in the global affairs of the entire world like no other nation.

Beyond that though, the United States is known for sending out more of God's ambassadors (missionaries) with the message of repentance and acceptance of Christ like no other country in history. Missions has become so much a part of the American Christian culture that we send out close to *two million Americans every year on overseas short-term mission teams.*

Clearly, *no one* sends out missionaries (messengers) like the United States.

Are we tall? Yes, Americans are known, like Germans, for being very tall compared to the other peoples of the world.

Smoothly shaven? Again, yes. Our men shave their faces, our women shave their legs, and now our young people are even shaving their entire bodies.

Whirring Wings

We skipped right over one of the most curious lines of the chapter, the first one:

> *"Woe to the land shadowed with buzzing [clashing] wings"*

Frankly, that part of the verse is so strange, it guarantees confusion.

Let's start by looking at what is obvious. The land has a lot of "wings" in it. A candidate nation has to have enough wings in it to make it stand out from other countries, or God wouldn't have bothered to note that as a distinguishing feature.

And these wings make loud noise.

The Hebrew word for "buzzing," or in some translations "whirring," is **tslatsal**, which elsewhere in the Bible is normally translated as a "cymbal" (yes, the clanging musical instrument). *Tslatsal* is the official Hebrew word for cymbal. In fact, Isaiah 18:1 is the *only* place in Scripture where that word is translated as "buzzing" or "whirring" instead of "clashing," "banging," or "clanging."

That is probably because modern biblical translators had in mind armies of locusts somewhere in Africa and so they stretched their translation to make that idea make sense since they couldn't imagine crashing or clanging locust wings.

However, if we don't try to force a translation and let the Hebrew say what it says, Isaiah has said *"Woe to the land of clanging wings…"*

The only possible understanding is flying things that make very loud noises as they fly.

There are only three possibilities of a land filled with wings anyway: birds, insects (locusts), or airplanes (and helicopters).

We can rule birds out. Their wings don't make much noise. And no country is known for being filled with tons of birds when compared with others.

We can say the same of locusts, and also add that any nation overwhelmed with armies of locusts by definition is not going to be prosperous but devastated by destruction to their food supply and other vegetation. It would be impossible for any nation to be militarily fearsome for generations while simultaneously being attacked by hordes of locusts that sap its economic strength.

Strong militaries and armies of locusts don't mix.

Plus, as we've already said, these wings make very *loud* crashing noises, they don't hum or buzz like locusts.

Aircraft on the other hand *do* make a lot of noise. Their engines are very loud, whether considering jet engines or whirring helicopter blades. Yet, Isaiah would have had no concept of modern aircraft. If God gave him a vision of an air force, he would not have known what he was seeing other than it was an army of flying things that made huge noises. *Clashing wings.*

How would this apply to the United States?

Russia has the *third* largest air force in the world with 3,200 active aircraft. The closest runners up after that are Israel and India, both of whom have fewer than 1,500.

The United States on the other hand has over *13,000 active aircraft and 9,000 military drones.* This is seven times what Russia has and twenty times everyone else. Not to mention the world's *second* largest air force is *also* an American air force with 4,400 retired aircraft sitting in a boneyard in the Arizona desert. And that's not our only aircraft boneyard!

So, we have two to three times more aircraft than Russia *just sitting in storage.*

With regards to commercial flights, American Airlines is the largest in the world with respect to fleet size, revenue, and passengers, but Delta Airlines is the largest in the world with respect to assets.[147]

Did you catch that? The two largest airlines in the world are both American. Actually, the *four largest* airlines in the world are all American. Together, American, Delta, United, and Southwest Airlines moved almost 700 million passengers in 2016, while China only moved 167 million that same year among all its airlines. (75% less). The top European airlines only moved 250 million passengers (63 % less).

Add to that the fact that 600,000 Americans currently hold active pilot licenses.

---

[147] https://en.wikipedia.org/wiki/World%27s_largest_airlines

REVELATION UNFOLDING

I will personally never forget certain radar images the newscasters kept showing on September 11th, 2001. Besides the horrifying sights of the Twin Towers collapsing from a million different angles, they showed before and after photos of U.S. air traffic on the national radar screens.

Once it was known the terrorists were using aircraft to attack us, President Bush ordered a complete halt to all air traffic across the nation. For the first time in our history since the invention of flight, no airplanes flew.

The radar image was nothing short of incredible. A dark screen with bright green dots *everywhere* was the before image. Every green dot represented a different aircraft and they literally were covering the entire United States, flying in every direction imaginable. Then, the time-lapsed video shows all the green dots disappearing as plane after plane lands until the airspace is completely clear. The change was dramatic.

More than any country, the United States is truly a nation whirring with wings.

Still, why does God single this characteristic out about the United States? There may be spiritual reasons for him calling out our aerospace industry in particular, but that may be a discussion for a different book.

Hollow Cylinders

There is another curious phrase we have not yet explored:

> *"Which sends ambassadors by sea,*
> *Even in vessels of reed on the water"*

Once more, Bible translators are stretching the words beyond reason to make sense of Hebrew that doesn't make sense if your mind is closed to unexpected possibilities.

First, the phrase "on the water" is misleading. The Hebrew literally says "over the surface of the water." The difference being there is no definite sense of these vessels touching the water. It could mean that, but it could also be argued the phrase is better translated as "above the surface of the water."

This is the sense of Genesis 1:2 where it says the Spirit was moving over the surface of the waters. Also, in Genesis 1:20, we see this word translated as "and let birds fly *above* the earth."

Also, the word translated as "even" is actually just an "and." So, it is more accurate to say, *"Which sends messengers by sea and in vessels of reed above the surface of the waters."*

Next, let's look at the word "vessel." From the English, we get the sense this means boat because we often use the word vessel in English to mean ship. Yet, the Hebrew word here is **biḵ·lî**. Nowhere else in Scripture is the word *bikli* ever translated as "boat" or "ship!" We have different Ancient Hebrew words for boats and ships, namely *oni* and *tsiy*.

Instead, everywhere else in Scripture, *bikli* refers to a long, hollow cylindrical object, usually a cup for drinking, or a jar or an urn to be used in the temple. The word truly means "vessel" as in vessels for eating or ritual use. Think of a metal martini shaker. That shape is a *bikli*.

You might ask, *can't Isaiah be using the word figuratively as we use the word vessel to describe a boat?* Not likely, because nowhere else in Scripture is the word used that way.

Beyond that, Isaiah uses a very strange modifier. He says these are vessels of "reed" or as some translations have it "papyrus."

So, hypothetically, there is a tiny possibility he is describing boats made of reeds like the ancient Egyptian reed boats. Yet, if we are honest does that really fit with the rest of the chapter? A boat made of reeds is pretty primitive and even in Isaiah's time it is hard to imagine a nation that is called militarily "fearsome since its beginning" being dependent on papyrus reed boats for its navy.

Isaiah was post-Solomon, who built massive ships of cedars and other timber. Reed boats would not be considered "fearsome." Furthermore, we know the prophecies of Isaiah 14 – 24 have not yet been fulfilled. They represent end-time prophecies, including Isaiah 18. No country today sends out messengers on boats made of bulrushes, much less a fearsome one.

And again, the word vessel should not be translated as boat. No, there has to be another reason he uses the phrase "hollow cylinders of reed."

He is either using the word "reed" for emphasis on the cylindrical nature of the vessel, or another sense of papyrus (paper) is meant.

If the second, then the lightweight nature or the vessel's skin would likely be in mind. Isaiah would have not known about aluminum or other lightweight materials used in aircraft, so given his limited vocabulary, calling them hollow cylinders of paper seems like a good attempt.

A Better Translation

Now, let's combine all we've learned about the original Hebrew, discard wrong preconceptions about what for some unexplained reason it should not mean, and see a more literal and accurate translation:

> *"Woe to the land of loud, crashing wings,*
> *Which lies on the other side of the waters of the black race,*
> *Which sends messengers/ambassadors by sea,*
> *And in papyrus hollow cylinders above the surface of the waters, saying,*
> *'Go swiftly, messengers, to a nation clean-shaven and tall,*
> *To a people fearsome from their beginning onward,*
> *A nation very firmly resolved,*
> *Whose land the rivers divide.'"*

The passage seems to make more sense now, and there is a lot of reason to believe it could be applying to the United States.

To sum up, here are the things the United States matches from this passage:

- America lies to the west of Africa
- The U.S. is known for its military might, it has never lost a war (Vietnam was an intentional pull-out for political reasons, not a loss)
- The U.S. has the largest air force in the world
- Americans are known for the missionaries (messengers) we send out all over the world.
- Americans are notably tall and clean-shaven compared with other peoples.
- Americans are a fiercely determined people. Culturally, we are firmly determined whenever we corporately set our minds to something.
- The United States is divided by the Mississippi and its tributaries.

We have so far limited the translation above to a good literal translation. Now, let's add a few more clarifying words to smooth it out that seem justified by the context and intent of the author:

> *"Woe to the land of loud, crashing wings,*
> *Which lies beyond the waters of the black races,*
> *Which sends missionaries by sea,*
> *And in lightweight hollow cylinders above the waters,*
> *Say, 'Return swiftly, missionaries, to a nation clean-shaven and tall,*
> *To a people militarily fearsome from their beginning onward,*

> *A nation very firmly resolved,*
> *Whose land the rivers divide.'"*

Once you let the Hebrew be translated in its most natural usage, the meaning becomes clear, and there are no other nations today that could match this description except for the United States.

Devastation by War

If God is speaking through Isaiah regarding the future of the United States, what is the nature of the warning? What does it mean for America?

Here's more of Isaiah 18:

> *"All inhabitants of the world and dwellers on the earth:*
> *When he lifts up a banner on the mountains, you see it;*
> *And when he blows a trumpet, you hear it.*
> *For so the Lord said to me,*
> *'I will take My rest,*
> *And I will look from My dwelling place*
> *Like clear heat in sunshine,*
> *Like a cloud of dew in the heat of harvest.'*
> *For before the harvest, when the bud is perfect*
> *And the sour grape is ripening in the flower,*
> *He will both cut off the sprigs with pruning hooks*
> *And take away and cut down the branches.*
> *They will be left together for the mountain birds of prey*
> *And for the beasts of the earth;*
> *The birds of prey will summer on them,*
> *And all the beasts of the earth will winter on them.'"*
> (Isaiah 18:3-6)

Once more, a very cryptic passage. However, what's not cryptic is the ending. Many people will be killed. Vultures and wild animals will feed on the unburied bodies for a year.

We're immediately hit with a million questions: What's happening *exactly*? *Why* is this happening? When does it happen? What causes all the killing?

We won't go into all the details of the Hebrew this time, but below is an attempt to smooth out some of the language in English to make the intent more understandable:

> *"All inhabitants of the world and dwellers on the earth:*
> *When he lifts up a flag on the mountains, Look!*
> *And when he blows a trumpet, Listen!*
> *For so the Lord said to me,*
> *'I will take My rest,*
> *And I will look on from My dwelling place*
> *And be like a mirage in the desert,*
> *Like shimmering vapor in the heat of harvest.'*
> *For before the harvest, when the bud is perfect*
> *And the unripe grape is ripening in the flower,*
> *He [GOD] will both cut off the sprigs with pruning hooks*
> *And take away and cut down the branches.*
> *They will be left together for the vultures*
> *And for the beasts of the earth;*
> *The birds of prey will summer on them,*
> *And all the beasts of the earth will winter on them.'"*

Let's go verse by verse to get the full meaning of what God is saying:

All inhabitants of the world and dwellers on the earth:

God is telling the whole world to pay attention and watch the judgment He is about to deal to the nation of Isaiah 18, presumably the United States. None of Isaiah's other prophetic pronouncements tell the whole world to watch what is about to happen.

This is further reinforcement that the country of Isaiah 18 is of high importance on the world scene as God is using it as a witness of his judgment to the world.

When he lifts up a flag on the mountains, Look!
And when he blows a trumpet, Listen!

This is an indication of the specific timing. God is telling the world that when a flag (or banner) is lifted up on the mountains, and when he blows a trumpet, that is when He will execute His judgment on the Isaiah 18 nation. (From this point forward, we will presume it to be the United States.)

Still a bit cryptic of course. Understanding there is a flag of some sort is easy, but which mountains? That would help us know which country's flag to look for too.

There are only two options: a flag posted on the mountains in the United States, or a flag posted on mountains in Israel.

A flag (standard) being posted in a place is a sign of change of governmental authority. To plant your flag is to take possession.

Either location is technically possible, but there are currently no scenarios that makes sense for the United States. The only two options would be a future war where the United States loses the Rocky Mountains and then retakes them, or a future war where we invade another nation and plant our flag on their mountains.

Both are possible, but don't sound likely. Remembering that the Bible is Israel-centric, the first possibility of a flag being planted on the mountains of Israel seems more plausible. Especially with the mention of the trumpet (*shofar*). Blowing the *shofar* (ram's horn trumpet) is a traditional Israeli practice accompanying ceremonial events.

Also, other Isaiah passages refer to a banner being placed on the mountains of Israel.

Today, all of the arguing and bickering about the conflict between Israel and the Palestinians centers around who has the right to govern the mountains of Israel, the West Bank. No modern voice, not even Israel itself, has yet officially declared that Israel has the unilateral right to govern those mountains – even though historically those mountains were the most Jewish of all territories and promised by God to His people – to the exclusion of the Palestinians.

If Israel, at some future date, whether unilaterally, or with the consent of other nations, declared itself to be in full final authority over the West Bank, Israeli flags would be raised in every city on those mountains, and such an event would clearly be celebrated with the sounding of many *shofars* (trumpets) across the land.

In May of 2018, thousands of teenagers performed an Israeli flag march through East Jerusalem[148] to declare Israel's sovereignty, and one month earlier, Israeli settlers protected by armed guards posted Israeli flags on top of Abraham's Tomb in Hebron.[149] These events are a foreshadowing of a future, much larger event.

Previously, we discussed how there will be some event that causes the Assyrian (likely Erdoğan) to say "let's go help the Children of Lot (Palestinians)."

Such a declaration by Israel to permanently and unilaterally annex the West Bank could indeed be the trigger. Perhaps this declaration is initiated due to encouragement from the United States? Or perhaps it is in spite of opposition from a future U.S. president who stands against Israel? (And so would be an additional reason for our judgment.)

Our best educated guess at this time is that Israel will declare itself sovereign over the West Bank, and Erdoğan will begin forming his coalition to stop it. When that happens, we should look for the terrible judgment on the United States to begin which will make us unable to help defend Israel.

> *For so the Lord said to me, "I will take My rest,*
> *And I will look on from My dwelling place*
> *And be like a mirage in the desert,*
> *Like shimmering vapor in the heat of harvest"*

Our history as Americans is strongly Christian and we've walked with God well in the past. The same cannot be said about us today at all. Look no further than the 60 million babies we've aborted on the sacrificial altar to our new God, the American Dream.

---

[148] https://www.haaretz.com/israel-news/.premium-thousands-participate-in-israeli-flag-march-through-jerusalem-1.6078170
[149] https://www.middleeastmonitor.com/20180417-settlers-place-israel-flag-over-ibrahimi-mosque/

In the days after September 11th, Americans came together in unity. Congressmen from both political parties stood on the steps of the Capitol building and spontaneously broke into song, singing God Bless America. People started showing up in churches with renewed fervor.

When the Isaiah 18 judgment comes, Americans will naturally seek God in desperation.

Unfortunately, what God is saying is that in that day, He will not help us – He will be like a mirage to us. It will seem like He is going to be there for us, but then, He will not. Just like a mirage. This is heartbreaking.

> ***For before the harvest, when the bud is perfect***
> ***And the unripe grape is ripening in the flower***

This part seems to be telling us more about *when* this judgment will happen. It is saying that the judgment will happen before the "harvest," and when grapes are still ripening in their flower.

In ancient Israel, the grape harvest started in early June and continued in July and August. Grapes flower approximately 3 to 4 months before they are harvested. So, while this is not an exact science, it would seem that the indicated time is probably early Spring, or maybe even early March.

It is unclear whether the harvest described is the grape harvest, the barley harvest, or the wheat harvest. Given the context, it would see the grape harvest is meant, though early to mid-March would also be before the barley and wheat harvests too.

We can also see spiritual meanings here. "Before the harvest" can mean "before the rapture" since the rapture is always referred to as a harvest.

This could be a corrective phrase to Americans since American Christians tend to believe the rapture is going to save them from experiencing any judgment.

Jesus said He was the Vine (grape vine), and we should abide in Him to bear much fruit. Therefore, the grape vine is a symbol for the church with Jesus as the central vine fueling all of the branches.

Many American pastors have said recently that they believe a revival is coming soon to the American church with many, many to be saved. This could be confirmation that this revival is indeed coming to the American church, but that unfortunately, it will not result in a delay of judgment – and that all the new believers will be cut off before they can bear fruit.

> *He [GOD] will both cut off the sprigs with pruning hooks*
> *And take away and cut down the branches.*

This is statement of judgment.

In the Bible, "to cut off" is a well-known euphemism for to kill.

While we could argue that the phrase "cut off" is being used metaphorically in conjunction with the image of a vine, the following verses referring to dead bodies eliminate that possibility.

No, God is going to allow a significant portion of the Isaiah 18 country, we believe the United States, to be killed.

Who will be killed? Both the *sprigs* and the *branches*. **Meaning children, young people, and adults.**

How many will be killed? Clearly unknown.

If we look at history, though, God has already executed judgment on the United States once before: The American Civil War.

God judged us then for the sin of enslaving 4 million black men, women, and children for economic gain. As a result, during the Civil War, almost 1 million white men died, more than all the other wars of the United States combined.

That represents 25% of those enslaved at the time. The number of slaves killed during their enslavement has been hard for historians to calculate. The number of slaves imported to the U.S. was only 470,000 [150], so the only way for that number to grow to 4 million in a half century or so was if the death rate was relatively low. If we assume 470,000 overall could have

---

[150] https://en.wikipedia.org/wiki/Slavery_in_the_United_States

been killed or suffered an early death from hard labor, then the number of men killed in the Civil War was double that.

However, God says in His law:

> *"He who strikes a man so that he dies shall surely be put to death."*
> *(Exodus 21:12)*
>
> *"He who kidnaps a man and sells him, or if he is found in his hand, shall surely be put to death."*
> *(Exodus 21:16)*
>
> *"And if a man beats his male or female servant with a rod, so that he dies under his hand, he shall surely be punished... you shall give life for life, eye for eye, tooth for tooth, hand for hand, foot for foot, burn for burn, wound for wound, stripe for stripe."*
> *(Exodus 21:20,23)*

So, perhaps the number of slaves killed was actually 1 million? Or maybe God took 500,000 lives to pay for the 500,000 sold into slavery and then another 500,000 for those who were unjustly killed?

Either way, God's law will not be thwarted. Restitution must be made.

We have no way of knowing what God intends to do in the future, He is a merciful God, but with the number of 60 million babies aborted looming over our nation, we should tremble remembering the numbers of God's past judgment.

Just as many Americans today scoff at the idea of abortion being sin, so back then did many Americans scoff at the idea of slavery being a sin. So, it doesn't matter what we think. It only matters what He thinks.

> *"They will be left together for the vultures*
> *And for the beasts of the earth;*
> *The birds of prey will summer on them,*
> *And all the beasts of the earth will winter on them."*

If we really dwell on this part of the prophecy, something stands out as strange. *Why* are these human bodies left out for an entire year? People typically don't leave the bodies of others lying about, unburied.

Even if the people don't care about them, just because of the stink and for health reasons they would bury or cremate them. During the Civil War, even with battles where tens of thousands of men died in a single day, people after the battle busied themselves with collecting and burying the bodies for those very reasons.

So, what possible reason could there be for this situation?

A few possibilities:

> 1.) *Everyone is killed, so no one is left to bury them.*
>
> This option is not plausible. Not only is it very difficult to kill *everyone* in a country, but the remaining parts of Isaiah 18 indicate there are survivors.
>
> 2.) *We are unable to reach many of the bodies.*
>
> This is possible. Both China and North Korea are known to have developed a warfare strategy against the United States that involves setting off EMP weapons over America, i.e. nuclear devices at a high altitude.[151]
>
> Doing such a thing creates a massive electro-magnetic pulse that would burn up electrical circuits everywhere. Airplanes would fall from the sky, the electrical grid would fail, cell phones and internet and computers would be gone, cars and trucks would be fried, and even water pumps would stop pumping.
>
> Perhaps we can't bury the bodies simply because we don't have the ability to communicate or easily transport ourselves to get them. We'd have a lot of other things to worry about.
>
> 3.) *We are unable to bury the bodies because of radiation.*

---

[151] https://geopoliticalfutures.com/emp-threat-works-means-korean-crisis/

If the United States were hit by full-blown nuclear blasts during a war, we would not be able to enter the affected areas to bury the bodies. Animals would be undeterred from entering, but people definitely could not go.

4.) *So many people are killed, the sheer number of bodies is just overwhelming for the remaining population.*

Back to the possibility of the EMP attack, George Friedman and Phillip Orchard of Geopolitical Futures have this to say:

> According to the 2008 report on critical infrastructure: "The cascading effects from even one or two relatively small weapons exploded in optimum location in space at present would almost certainly shut down an entire interconnected electrical power system, perhaps affecting as much as 70 percent or possibly more of the United States, all in an instant .... Should significant parts of the electrical power infrastructure be lost for any substantial period of time, the Commission believes that the consequences are likely to be catastrophic, and many people may ultimately die for lack of the basic elements necessary to sustain life in dense urban and suburban communities."
>
> The following year, the chairman of the EMP Commission told Congress that the damage in areas within the blast radius would be an order of magnitude worse than what Hurricane Katrina inflicted on the Gulf Coast in 2005—and that a 90% fatality rate nationwide within a year due to starvation and systems breakdown was plausible.
>
> Since then, public officials, including a former CIA director, have routinely given credence to the 90% figure ...

The idea of an EMP attack is only a possibility, but whatever happens, Isaiah 18 is telling us that something is so devastating that both children and adults are killed and the bodies are unable to be buried.

If we look back at the Civil War for a moment, the punishment fit the crime. Almost literally, an eye for an eye was exacted as not only the numbers matched.

Many of the deaths in the Civil War were actually caused by sickness rather than violence, and one of the top causes of death for African slaves was sickness on the slave ships bringing them to the Americas. On those ships, the death rate was very high, and bodies were tossed overboard.

So, slaves died from sickness and violence and were often buried in unmarked graves. And white Civil War soldiers died from sickness and violence and were often buried in unmarked graves.

When it comes to abortion, we don't bury the bodies. The tiny babies so brutally aborted are tossed by abortion clinics into the trash without burial.

So, it seems that, like the Civil War, our coming judgment may match the crime. If I were a betting man, I would bet on at least 60 million people killed and left largely unburied, and they will probably be concentrated in those states that had the highest abortion rates.

There is one positive note from God's description of His action. He says that He will "cut off the sprigs with pruning hooks." He does not say He will kill the vine. To prune a plant is typically done for its own health. Yes, sometimes the pruning needed is drastic, and it takes a while to see the restored growth, but when the plant does grow back, it's healthier than ever.

Terms of Endearment

There is some more good news. One unique feature of this prophetic passage is the very first word: Woe.

Instead of just saying "To the land of loud, crashing wings," God says, "*Woe*, to the land of loud, crashing wings." Numerous scholars have pointed out that the word "woe" is not used with any of the surrounding prophetic passages about other nations.

Woe is a term of lament, and since it is not said to the other nations, the best understanding is that God cares specially about the country of Isaiah 18. The people who are about to be judged/pruned are dear to His heart.

We can see this also when He says that He will be like a mirage to the people. Meaning, this is a people that has it in them to seek the true God of the Bible when they are in trouble, but that He will not be there for them this time when they reach out.

We see more evidence of the specialness of this country to God in the final part of Isaiah 18:

> *"In that time **a present** will be brought to the Lord of Hosts*
> *From a nation clean-shaven and tall,*
> *And from a people militarily fearsome from their beginning onward,*
> *A nation very firmly resolved, whose land the rivers divide—*
> ***To the place of the name of the Lord of Hosts,***
> ***To Mount Zion."***

The word "present" means a gift of homage – an honoring gift to God or a king. This section proves that the nation of Isaiah 18 will not be completely destroyed in this judgment but will recover.

It also shows that this nation is special in that it has a heart for God. It brings a special gift of homage to Jesus in Jerusalem *after* receiving its judgment. So, the heart response of the people after being judged is repentance, humility, and a love and respect for God.

This is why God says to them "Woe." He does not take pleasure in their destruction, He loves them, but justice and judgment must occur for their preservation and perfection.

Of course, we believe that the nation of Isaiah 18 is the United States and these additional pieces of information only solidify that interpretation.

The United States was the second nation in the history of the world to be officially consecrated to God in a ceremony involving the entire U.S. government right after the adoption of the U.S. constitution and the inauguration of George Washington. (Interestingly, the consecration ceremony took place at Ground Zero of the 9/11 attack.)

The United States is very special to God among the nations. We are not better than other nations. Again, the United States is not *better*. Special does not mean better, it means set aside for a special purpose.

Among all the nations throughout the history of the world, few countries as a whole have sought God and worked to serve Him and His purposes like the United States. Our missionary and church planting activity dwarfs the efforts of all other singular nations. Historically, America has aspired to a higher morality than any other nation, though admittedly this has diminished greatly in recent generations.

We are not perfect, but He loves us. He doesn't love us because of what we've done. On the contrary, we've only been able to do what we've done because He loved us and chose us first for special purposes, to be a City on the Hill, to be a Free Nation established on God's principles.

Yet, now we have turned our back on Him. And so, the chastisement comes. Because God chastises those He loves.

What Gift Is Brought?

So, what is the "present" that is so noteworthy it is revealed to Isaiah. It's a worshipful gift, but what exactly could the gift be?

> *"In that time **a present** will be brought to the Lord of Hosts From a nation clean-shaven and tall…to the place of the name of the Lord of Hosts, To Mount Zion."*

It seems to be a gift that is given once the Messiah has taken His throne in Jerusalem. The passage says that we not only take it to Jerusalem, but to the Lord of Hosts, Himself.

So, we bring this present after the Tribulation is finished and the antichrist is defeated and killed.

It does not seem to be the kind of financial tribute a subjugated nation would typically bring to a conquering king. Of course, it *could* be, but if it were just an annual tribute, it seems like the description would be more like "From that time forward, this people will bring a yearly gift to the Lord of Hosts."

Also, during the Millennial Reign of Christ, financial tributes will almost certainly be the norm with every nation in the world regularly bringing tribute to Jesus. If so, then a tribute like that would not be noteworthy enough to mention as a prominent point for the future of the United States.

This definitely seems like a single, special gift.

What that gift could be is a complete mystery. The only gift biblically speaking that could seem to stand out enough to fit this level of importance is the Ark of the Covenant.

However, we should say clearly that such an idea is highly speculative and outside of Indiana Jones movies, we have absolutely no evidence at all that the United States government is in possession of the Ark.

Nevertheless, it is an interesting theory. The Ark of the Covenant is the holiest relic in Scripture and has been missing for 2,500 years. No other biblical object seems significant enough to match the gift of Isaiah 18, assuming it is a physical and not a spiritual gift.

Strong cases have been made that the Knights Templar could have rediscovered the Ark under the Temple Mount in the Middle Ages. It is also known that the Knights Templar morphed into the Masonic Lodge at the end of the Middle Ages, and that later by the 20th century the power center of the Masonic Lodge had transferred from Britain to the United States.

So, who knows?

The Great Pacific War

In summary, Isaiah 18 is likely an end-times prophecy about the United States. The best interpretation tells us that God cares about us, but that we are due for judgment. Our best guess is that when Israel officially plants its flags over the West Bank and the antichrist launches his coalition, the United States will experience a severe and swift destruction of many people, not just our military, but children too.

The destruction will happen in such a way that the bodies of many people will not be buried for a long time.

With a country the size of the United States, there are only a few ways to affect the entire people so devastatingly: conquest by foreign armies, biological (disease), chemical weapons, nuclear weapons, EMP weapons, famine, or natural disasters.

Conquest by foreign soldiers would not target the children equally with the adults. It would be heavy on adults with women and children only hurt as collateral damage because the goal would be conquest.

Chemical weapons are too difficult to disperse over such a large area, so that is ruled out.

The Book of Zechariah says the plague horse goes south to Africa, and the judgment of Isaiah 18 seems much too sudden for it to be a plague, so in spite of Coronavirus, we can probably rule out biological.

Famine would also be much too slow – people would be able to bury victims of starvation – and anyway, the black horse (famine) goes north to Europe and Russia.

Natural disasters are possible, but they would have to be severe and widespread and of multiple kinds at the same time to create this level of destruction on the United States. There are indeed many natural disasters predicted in Revelation, so it's possible, but we believe less probable than acts of war.

Both nuclear weapons and EMP attacks remain the most likely candidates.

When Jesus breaks the second seal, the red horsemen rides to the far east and roams the world. Any war involving the countries of Eastern Asia would by default draw the United States in.

Of course, there are other mentions of "banners" being planted in other chapters of Isaiah that seem to be referring to the moment of the Second Coming of Christ, so it's also possible this destruction occurs at the same time as the Battle for Armageddon.

However, at this time, the best guess as to when this judgment will happen to America is when the 2nd Seal is broken. During that war.

Final Note:

As I write this (August 2020), both a civil war and a war with China are seeming increasingly likely. Most of this book was written years ago including this section on the war for the United States. However, it is now more real than ever.

In very recent news, the leadership of the Democrat party met to "war game" the election. The result of their games? They intentionally provoked a civil war ...[152]

---

[152] https://spectator.us/top-democrats-contemplate-civil-war-biden-loses/

THE 3rd SEAL

FAMINE/ECONOMIC DEVASTATION

"When He opened the third seal, I heard the third living creature say, "Come and see." So, I looked, and behold, a black horse, and he who sat on it had a pair of scales in his hand. And I heard a voice in the midst of the four living creatures saying, "A quart of wheat for a denarius, and three quarts of barley for a denarius; and do not harm the oil and the wine." (Revelation 6:5-6)

WHEN JESUS breaks the third seal, the black horse rides. There are two possible ways to view the results of Jesus breaking the 3rd seal. Some scholars see a prediction of terrible famine, others see a severe economic depression.

The high price of wheat and barley as it reads argues in favor of *famine*, but the "unharmed" oil and wine argue against it. Curiously, the high price of wheat and barley could also be used to argue *economic depression*, while the untouched prices of oil and wine say no to that too.

The phrase "do not harm the oil and the wine" implies the wheat and barley will be "harmed." That means this is not a general economic depression – at least it doesn't *begin* with an economic depression – but if the price of wheat and other grains skyrocket, then the cost of living for everyone will skyrocket, which will necessarily result in an economic depression.

Famines are typically caused by three things: drought, crop disease or other blight, or the actions of men/governments.

A general drought would harm everything, including both the olive oil and wine production, so that cannot be the issue, unless the drought occurs in regions of the world that grow wheat and barley, but not where there are cultivations of olive trees and grape vines.

Seems like we need to know *where* this will happen.

Where Does the Black Horse Go?

Let's recall Zechariah 6:6:

> *"The one with the black horses is going to the north country..."*

Meaning, north from Israel: Europe & Russia. Whatever this judgment means, it is certainly going to happen in Europe.

What the angel says is that a *choenix* of wheat will be sold for a "denarius" and three *choenixes* of barley will be sold for the same. These are ancient measures and ancient coins. We need to modernize the amounts for our own understanding.

A *choenix* is almost a quart, so the text is saying that a quart of wheat will be sold for a denarius. Today, wheat is typically sold in bushels, and one bushel equals 32 quarts.

Current market prices are around $4.90 for a bushel of wheat. So, a quart of wheat currently costs 15 cents on the commodity market. (If an end/retail consumer wants to buy a quart of wheat, however, it will cost them about $2.50)

Important: Please note that a loaf of bread at the supermarket costs approximately 20 times the cost of a quart of wheat on the commodity market.

Yet, how much is a Denarius?

A Denarius was a small silver coin containing 3.4 grams of silver. At the time of this writing, silver is selling for $0.84 per gram, so the value of silver in a denarius coin if melted down would net $2.85.

Now, that doesn't sound like a lot. $0.15 for a quart of wheat up to $2.85?

Yet, a loaf of bread is 20 times the cost of the raw wheat, so the price of a loaf bread in this scenario would jump to about $57! Three loaves of bread per week and the average family would be spending $600 - $800 per month just on bread.

It doesn't end there because the cost of everything else grain-related would go up too. Pastas, pastries, even animal feed…yes, animal feed would suddenly shoot high, so the price of meat would also be astronomical.

It Gets Worse

Valuing a Denarius at a $2.85 is not the best interpretation. That is the *lowest* we could value it actually. Just a few years ago, silver was much more costly, which would make a loaf of bread approach $150.

The worse news is the meaning of "Denarius" (root of the Spanish *dinero*) literally means "daily wage." A Denarius was what a worker was typically paid for a day's worth of work.

One reason being that a worker could take 3 grams of silver out of the ground with a day's labor. However, today we have sophisticated machinery that has dropped the price of silver dramatically in relation to a worker's daily wage.

Since the black horse rides to Europe, we need to look at the average daily wage in those countries to figure this out better. The typical European worker, averaged over all the countries on that continent, is approximately $2,500 per month (net after taxes), or $100 per day.

This is probably the best number to work with according to the intent of Scripture: **A quart of wheat for a day's wages.**

Which means that a bushel of wheat would sell for $3,200!

One bushel of wheat produces about 70 loaves of bread. That would mean each loaf of bread would be $46 just in material cost. After distribution, production, and retail, there would be no way to produce a loaf of bread for less than $150 - $200 and retail prices could easily approach $900 or more.

Of course, in these situations, people would stop buying bread at grocery stores. They would begin milling grain at home and baking their own bread. They would even start growing their own wheat in their back yards when possible. Anything to save money.

But Why Would This Happen?

Now, what could possibly have such a dramatic impact on the wheat market to drive up prices in this way?

The United States currently produces 2 billion bushels of wheat per year and keeps 1 billion in storage at any given time. Recently, there was concern that the United States was going to dip into its wheat storage a bit by about 100 million bushels. Just the risk of that had people talking about a jump in U.S. wheat price from $3.90 to $5.00 per bushel.

100 million bushels may sound like a lot, but it is *not*. That only represents 0.37% of the world's production each year. *That's right, just the threat of a reduction of 1/3 of 1% of the world's supply caused wheat prices to go up by 25%.*

Now, remembering that the 3rd seal is broken after the 2nd seal, what would happen to the world's wheat production if the Great Pacific War we predicted earlier were to break out?

Together, the United States, India, China, and Australia produce 40% of the world's wheat production. If a great war were to destroy the wheat production in those countries or even just restrict delivery to the global market from these countries, wheat prices would shoot through the roof!

Europe and Russia produce another 30% of the world's wheat market, but suddenly that 30% would have to cover 70% of the world's demand. Untenable.

What would European commodity brokers do in a situation like that? Would they save their wheat supplies for the people of their own countries to make sure everyone had enough? No, they would make themselves rich by selling to the highest bidder, and the poor and middle class of Europe would have to do without.

So many agricultural and food industries would be upset that economic devastation would be a certainty.

Why Is Barley Different?

A superficial reading of the black horse passage leaves the reader with the simple impression that some kind of famine or economic problems will happen, but they don't understand why or where.

Yet, perhaps Scripture is telling us exactly where and why by mentioning those specific foods and how they're impacted?

In today's market, both wheat and barley are about the same price per bushel. Yet, the angel of Revelation 6 says barley is not affected as badly as wheat.

In the market described in Revelation where wheat is selling for $3,200 per bushel, the stated price of barley would be around $1,070 per bushel. Still crazy, but more affordable.

Barley loaves in a grocery store would run 1/3 of wheat loaves, at about $40 - $60 per loaf.

If our theory regarding the Great Pacific War is true, then this phenomenon with the barley is perfectly explained.

While Europe & Russia only produce 30% of the world's wheat production, *they produce 60% of the global barley supply.* And while the U.S., China, India, and Australia produce 40% of the world's wheat, *they only supply 12% of the global barley stocks.*

In other words, in a war affecting Asia and America, but not Europe & Russia, wheat would be very hard to come by. Barley would also be affected, not nearly as badly. A war involving the Asian powers and the

United States could very easily provoke skyrocketing wheat prices combined with elevated barley prices that aren't quite as bad.

Don't Touch the Oil & the Wine

The word "oil" means olive oil. The top three producers of olive oil in the world are Spain, Italy and Greece. Together they produce 75% of the world's olive oil supply. The other 25% is produced in North Africa and the Middle East. All of these regions would be untouched by a Chinese-American war, and the primary consumers of olive oil are in these same regions, so in our scenario, the price of olive oil would be untouched.

With regards to wine, the United States, China & Australia account for 17% of the world's wine production. Untouched areas produce 84%.

About 70% is produced in Europe (Just France, Spain & Italy together produce 50% of the world supply). So, if supply from the countries touching the Pacific Ocean were interrupted, the impact on the global market would be minimal.

Furthermore, those same Asian and American countries *consume* over 25% of the world's wine each year. In other words, countries involved in a potential Chinese-American War consume *more* wine than they produce. That mean if their consumers were removed from the picture, wine prices would actually go down, not up.

It Makes Sense

So, it turns out God is telling us more than we thought about the breaking of the 3rd Seal. By the specific products mentioned, He is giving us clear indicators of where and why these economic problems begin.

For example, if a drought struck Europe and caused a famine, the impact on the world's markets would be the *opposite* of what Scripture describes. In that scenario, it would be oil and wine supplies that would be devastated.

Their prices would skyrocket, but barley would be just moderately impacted, and wheat hardly at all.

On the other hand, destructive events to the U.S. and Asia would cause the exact ratios of harm to the grain markets predicted without touching the oil and the wine.

It seems God, through the 3rd seal, could be confirming the destination of the 2nd seal's red horse: The Ends of the Earth.

A Nuclear War?

Earlier, we hypothesized that the devastation predicted for the United States could be due to either nuclear explosions or EMP weapons.

The wheat shortage caused by the black horse may be telling us which it is. Below is a map of current wheat production centers of the world:

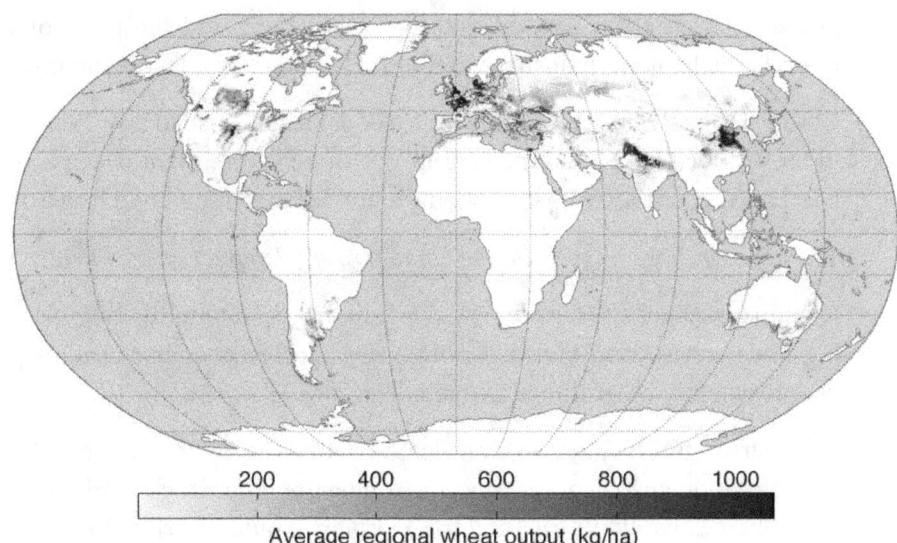

Note that the heaviest green areas in the United States are in the Midwest, right where all of our nuclear silos are. The heaviest green in India is in the north, right where many of India's military bases are and where they have nuclear weapons positioned against Pakistan.

The wheat production in China is heavily concentrated around Beijing (the capital), many of its other most populated cities, and near North Korea. These areas are also the most likely targets for a nuclear strike by us.

In other words, if the Great Pacific War turned nuclear on a large scale, the wheat production specifically of those countries would be badly affected.

The Impact

According to Investopedia, there are seven commodities that greatly affect the global stock markets if they have unexpected price fluctuations: Wheat, corn, oil, cotton, lumber, coffee, and gold.[153]

The price of lumber affects the cost of construction. Oil price jumps raise the cost of *everything* because of the increased transportation costs. Cotton prices determine the cost of clothing everywhere, and the price of gold impacts the banking industry and the stock market as a whole directly.

Corn is important because it's a basic foodstuff and is also now being used in the production of gasoline (ethanol). Coffee is important because of the number of countries whose economies are dependent on good harvests.

Yet, none of those have quite the same power to impact us as wheat.

If lumber skyrockets, people just stop building for a time. If cotton is crazy high, we can wait to buy more clothes. If coffee goes bananas, or gold, people just buy other things. Nobody starves.

Of course, oil is huge. If oil leapt from $70 to $3,000 per barrel, transportation costs would rise catastrophically high, stock markets would crash, barges wouldn't sail, and truck drivers wouldn't drive. In effect, the economy would lock down.

---

[153] https://www.investopedia.com/articles/economics/08/commodity-market-move.asp

Yet, long before the price of oil reached that height, corporations and governments everywhere would be rushing to drill new oil wells and build new pipelines. In a crisis like that, people have a way of rising to the occasion. Like an army of ants, they move mountains together that would be impossible to do alone from sheer determination. As oil spiked, new supplies would come online, and the price would stabilize again. It might go crazy for a time, but even in a worst-case scenario, prices would never reach those insane levels.

Wheat, on the other hand, cannot be recovered so quickly. It takes a full year to sow and harvest a new crop. And that's plenty of time for people to starve.

If oil impacts the fuels of cars and trucks and boats, wheat impacts the fuel of every worker that loads and unloads those cars and trucks and boats and makes the products carried by them.

Biblical commentators have pointed out that wheat and barley are basic foodstuffs that everyone consumes, and olive oil and wine are luxury items. This could be an indication that the poor and lower middle classes will suffer the most, but the wealthy will remain unaffected.

More wheat is traded on the world markets than all other crops combined[154] and it is the leading source of vegetal protein for people world-wide. In Europe, over 40% of wheat is used for animal feed, so the cost of eggs, milk and meat would skyrocket too.[155]

Here's what this would look like: Jean lives in France during this future time. He suddenly can no longer afford the baguette loaves he and his culture have loved for so long. He can't afford beef, or chicken, or pork products. But he also can't afford milk or cheese.

He can only afford fruits and vegetables and wine. Which means he is a forced Vegan, *but without the ability to consume wheat for protein.* Vegans *have* to supplement with some kind of protein, and wheat is the most popular choice.

---

[154] http://www.fao.org/docrep/006/y4011e/y4011e04.htm#bm04
[155] https://www.feedipedia.org/node/223

Thankfully, the few barley loaves he can afford help with this, but he would still struggle with protein deficiency. This kind of diet can cause severe health problems, even including starvation and death.[156] [157]

If Europe and Russia experience sudden, dramatic, and long-term increases in wheat cost, the overall impact would crush the public. First, low and middle-class Europeans would scramble to find alternatives to breads. Then, as they became unable to afford meats, milks, and eggs, they would become increasingly alarmed, agitated, and unstable.

At first, only the young and elderly would begin to pass away due to the dietary restrictions, while the rest would feel oppressed. Then, as the sharp jump in cost of food worked its way through the economy, there would be a dramatic shock to the European financial system, resulting in inflation and higher prices on everything.

Since the economic chaos would be caused by skyrocketing food prices, many people would likely begin to starve to death.

---

[156] https://www.nytimes.com/2007/05/21/opinion/21planck.html
[157] https://www.healthy-eating-support.org/not-enough-protein.html

THE 4th SEAL

PLAGUE

"When He opened the fourth seal, I heard the voice of the fourth living creature saying, 'Come and see.' So, I looked, and behold, a pale horse. And the name of him who sat on it was Death, and Hades followed with him." (Revelation 6:7-8a)

"...the dappled [horses] are going toward the south country." (Zechariah 6:6)

SCHOLARS UNIVERSALLY INTERPRET the 4th horseman of Revelation as representing plague because of the horse's color and because of the pestilence mentioned in the second part of Revelation 6:8.

In the verses above, the word "pale" in Revelation (Greek), and the word "dappled" in Zechariah (Hebrew), are both describing the same color: a sickly, mottled, ash-grey, like the color of skin on a dead person. Greek historians even used the word *chloros* (pale) to describe the appearance of people infected with the plague.[158]

The 4th Horseman Is *Not* Coronavirus

At this point, everybody is well familiar with the pestilence of Coronavirus. It has impacted everyone across the globe and devastated the economies of

---

[158] https://www.biblestudytools.com/commentaries/revelation/revelation-6/revelation-6-8.html

every country. Lockdowns and protests are rampant. There is a temptation to believe Coronavirus is the fulfilment of the 4th horsemen, but it isn't. First, in the verses above we see that Death and Hades follow the horseman. This does not match Coronavirus which has a fairly weak death rate, just a little worse than the flu. No, the plague that is represented by the pale horse is not just economically devastating or fear-inspiring, it will have a huge mortality rate. Wherever it goes, death follows. We can't say that about Coronavirus. This plague will be much worse.

It is much more fitting to ascribe Coronavirus as fulfilling a different prophecy Jesus gave:

> *"There will be great earthquakes, famines and* **pestilences** *in various places, and fearful events and great signs from heaven."* (Luke 21:11)

His prediction of pestilences combined with the others is about general signs of the end the whole world experiences, i.e. "labor pains" if you will. The 4th horseman is a much greater plague.

Second, Coronavirus has plagued the entire world, but Revelation 6th says that the pale horse will only have authority over 25% of the earth. Furthermore, Zechariah says the "dappled" horse goes south.

The Plague Goes to Africa

War to Asia and the Americas, famine to Europe, the antichrist to the Middle East, and the plague goes south.

And Africa already has large problems with disease (not just Coronavirus).

Of the top 10 worst pandemics so far in the 21st century, 7 of them happened in Africa. Of the epidemics in the last twenty years that have taken more than 4,000 lives, *almost 100% of them were in Africa* (with the sole exception being the Cholera outbreak in Haiti after their catastrophic earthquake in 2010).

So, when the Bible tells us that the plague horse goes south to Africa, it really shouldn't be a surprise.

Just a few years ago, there was a major Ebola outbreak in West Africa that took almost 30,000 lives. In 2013, a Yellow Fever outbreak took 45,000 lives, with 90% of them being in Africa.

In late 2017, the *Plague* itself, meaning the *Bubonic* Plague, broke out in Madagascar because people were digging up the dead bodies of their relatives and dancing with them in ceremonies.[159]

In 2018, Ebola broke out again, and locals refused to let doctors quarantine the patients or even treat them.[160]

Yet, why is disease so prevalent in Africa?

There are several reasons, chief among them being:

1.) Low access to clean water in villages
2.) General poor hygiene among large groups of the population
3.) No inhibition against eating strange meats (bats, rodents, monkeys)
4.) High levels of sexual promiscuity
5.) Strong superstitions discouraging the seeking of healthcare

It is important to say that historically, cultures who have worked to follow God's law as stated in the Bible have always eliminated these problems.

The Bible lays down some pretty clear dietary guidelines and strongly discourages us from eating the very meats that make Africans sick. Judeo-Christian cultures also tend to be very clean cultures.

The Bible teaches us that the only permissible sex is within a healthy heterosexual marriage and that divorce is to be avoided. If a culture follows this, AIDS and other STDs are eliminated.

In spite of what modern liberalism would have us believe, wherever cultures adopt the Bible as their foundation, rationalism is embraced and

---

[159] https://nypost.com/2017/10/26/madagascar-plague-linked-to-ritual-dance-with-dead-bodies/
[160] https://www.timeslive.co.za/news/africa/2018-05-22-superstition-stopping-ebola-victims-from-seeking-medical-care/

science flourishes. That is because the faith of the Bible is a rational faith that despises myth and superstition. Jews and Christians worship an All-Powerful God who cannot be controlled through ritual. The Bible teaches us that all wisdom and knowledge come from God, which leads us to understand it is good to seek knowledge and wisdom, which results in scientific pursuits. As a result, we seek healthcare, we don't avoid it.

That means that four of the five factors above would be eliminated just by following God's law.

Even the low access to water is fixed when a culture is permeated with biblical teaching. 4,000 years ago, men dug wells *by hand* in the Middle East to provide water for their families and their villages.

These were villages similar in size and ability to the poorest African tribes today. Bedouins of the ancient Middle East had no modern equipment, and they had no money. These weren't ancient armies digging these wells, but small villages.

Africans are not weaker or less intelligent than other peoples, nor do they have fewer resources. Africa is actually rich with resources (and no, they're not under the control of colonists).

The Bible encourages a strong work ethic many African tribal communities have yet to adopt. Instead, many hold a fatalistic, cyclical view of the world that says nothing can really be improved, so why try? This author has worked directly with the Maasai tribe of Africa (very representative) and encountered this well-known culture first-hand.

But Isn't Africa Christian Now?

The answer is yes ... but also not yet.

Over the past 150 years, the Gospel has indeed expanded across Sub-Saharan Africa at a rapid pace and Jesus has established churches in all of its countries. The number of new Christians has been dramatic and explosive.[161]

However, cultural transformation does not end with the establishment of churches. It *begins* with it. Once a people group has decided to submit themselves to the authority of Christ, it takes generations and generations for the full teaching of God's Word to sink in and permeate a culture. It took 1,100 years for Christianity to fully transform Europe out of the Dark Ages, and then another 500 to correct sins like the Crusades, the Inquisition, and other bad medieval happenings until reaching the Reformation. And even then, it still took longer to abolish slavery and other injustices.

While the Crusades and the Inquisition are pointed at as evidence of Christianity being barbaric at times, those events are actually pointed at because they stand out so much from the rest of history. Prior to Christianity, murderous wars and tortuous persecution of foreigners was quite commonplace among pagan peoples, so much so it was never noteworthy. Just expected.

With the slow growth of Christianity (often limited by the slow spread of literacy), over the centuries, schools, orphanages, and hospitals were established. History is filled with stories of saints who gave themselves away sacrificially in order to serve the poor and needy in imitation of Christ. The Inquisition, then, was actually an aberration that did not match the spirit of Jesus at all and was conducted by power-hungry men who called themselves by His name but didn't know Him at all.

Over the course of history, we see the slow march of progress and improvement, all due to the influence of Christianity.

With the invention of the printing press and now the internet, cultural transformation can happen much faster now, but it still takes generations.

African Christians are still in a very new phase. Many currently view the purpose of the Gospel and Christianity to be for their personal betterment and enrichment, not necessarily for their humbling and transformation.

---

[161] https://www.christianity.com/church/church-history/timeline/2001-now/the-explosion-of-christianity-in-africa-11630859.html

Ntozakhe Cezula, a professor from Stellenbosch University, has published a very in-depth article on that very topic (referenced here).[162]

In general (and we mean in *general*, not always), many African Christians can be more preoccupied with getting wealthy than they are with making sure that they are honoring God with their work and money. These simply have an immature outlook – it takes time to develop a more mature culture under the Gospel's influence.

The approach to Scripture is also often a selfish one. The Bible is not read privately in Africa with a concern for proper interpretation methods. Instead politicians and pastors publicly interpret it on behalf of the people, for the people, so they don't have to think for themselves (think medieval Catholic Church). And when read in private homes, it's not read for the purpose of correction and self-reformation, but the reader feels free to twist the text in whatever way suits their needs.

As Professor Cezula says:

> When African people read the Bible, a "dislocation" occurs and emphasis is not placed on the text's meaning *in itself but* rather on the meaning the text has for *the people reading it.*[163]

Not to beat a dead horse, but this is the reason the Bible has not yet had a transformative impact on African culture in a way that improves health and the quality of life for all.

The Other Horsemen Kill Africa's Hopes for Help

From the World Health Organization to Christian Medical Missionaries, recent outbreaks of Ebola, Yellow Fever, and the Black Plague in Africa have only been stopped by Herculean efforts from western medical

---

[162] http://www.scielo.org.za/scielo.php?script=sci_arttext&pid=S2413-94672015000200008
[163] http://www.scielo.org.za/scielo.php?script=sci_arttext&pid=S2413-94672015000200008

professionals to quarantine, treat and save as many people as they could, even at risk to their own lives.

Imagine a world that has already been rocked by a Great Pacific War, where possibly hundreds of millions are dying, and famine has devastated Europe with millions more starving to death. In such a world, the Red Cross, the World Health Organization, Doctors Without Borders, and all the other medical societies would already be taxed beyond their abilities.

Funding, personnel, and time would be severely limited and generally unavailable. There just aren't enough doctors to go around. Because the other devastations happen first, doctors and nurses would already be overwhelmed in their home countries. In that kind of a world, who would be left to help stave off an epidemic in Africa?

Very few or none is the answer.

And so, this time, the plague would go unchecked.

The only possible response of the nations of the world would be to quarantine the entire continent of Africa. Flights to and from will be blocked or heavily scrutinized for the infected. Navies will stop boats leaving the African shore.

No longer will refugees be welcome in Europe.

SPIRITUAL REASONS FOR GOD'S JUDGMENTS

THE FOUR HORSEMEN show us that God is not showing any favorites. No single continent or culture is being singled out or omitted – and all are being judged heavily!

> *"And power was given to them [each of the horsemen] over a fourth [25%] of the earth, to kill with sword, with hunger, with death, and by the beasts of the earth."*
> *(Revelation 6:8b)*

Every part of the world will be affected by the time Jesus finishes breaking the four seals. On the most basic level, we know this is just because all men and women are sinners.

- United States: War Devastation
- China: War Devastation
- Europe: Economic Devastation & Famine
- Africa: Plague(s) Leading to Death
- Middle East: Oppression Under the antichrist
- Israel: Conquest by the antichrist

Yet, do we see a reason God has chosen these particular judgments for these parts of the world?

As an **American**, I can say categorically that we Americans have become quite arrogant about ourselves and our abilities as a people. Our sense of self-importance is far too high. We put a *lot* of faith in ourselves, in our ability to overcome any obstacle as a people. There's a lot of ego wrapped up in it.

Even as I write this, I find myself unbelieving that America could ever lose a war. The United States military defeated? Ha! That's a riot. Tell me another one.

That kind of self-sufficiency and self-reliance is the enemy of dependence on God. Our strength and abilities have become our god.

Therefore, God will judge our god and show us how weak and insufficient we are through defeat in war and an inability to even bury our own dead.

We also as a culture have become very materialistic and worship money. Therefore, I believe a great loss of wealth will also affect the United States.

China has a similar self-confidence driven by intense ego. Internally, they are actually quite insecure, but they intend to solve that insecurity by eventually conquering the world and dominating all other races.

China's god is ego and power, so God will judge them and take away their power through devastation by war.

Recent diplomatic battles between the United States and Europe over the Iran deal reveals just how much **Europe** worships money. To European leaders, it does not matter if the Iranian government is evil and oppressive of its people. It does not matter if they develop nuclear weapons and missiles, even if they are making realistic threats about nuking Israel once they do.

No, the only thing that matters to European leaders is that they be able to keep selling things to the evil Iranian government because they want the money. Their businesses need the money. That is all that matters.

See this article if you'd like to read more about that particular topic: https://www.jpost.com/Diaspora/US-officials-on-roadshow-to-cut-Iran-investment-trade-sources-559319

Just as Americans trust in their military and that will be taken away, so will their economic abilities be taken away from Europeans. They won't even be able to afford bread.

I don't know that I've ever heard it put this clearly, but **Africans** worship their own personal vitality, meaning everything from sexual prowess to personal prosperity to health and wellness.

This explains every issue with their culture. Albinos are killed because their body parts are believed to bring wealth and good luck. Promiscuity is rampant because demonstrating sexual prowess is all-important, not so much obedience to God's law. The prosperity Gospel is adopted rather than the real Gospel because wealth, not transformation and repentance, is desired.

So, since Africans worship their own vitality, seeking life through it, God will instead bring them disease leading to death.

Muslims are passionate about rejecting the "oppression" of the Jewish people (we don't agree with their feeling on the matter), and they view submitting to the God of the Bible as an extension of that oppression, not realizing how blind they are – that they are actually rejecting freedom from oppression through restoration to their Creator.

So, God will let them instead be oppressed by the very mahdi they have longed for.

Israelis also put a lot of faith in their military today. It could be said that too many Israelis trust more in their military for security than God Himself.

So, God will allow a slow conquest by the antichrist to eliminate that self-reliance and slowly purify their trust in Him.

The 5th Seal

MARTYRDOMS

"When He opened the fifth seal, I saw under the altar the souls of those who had been slain for the word of God and for the testimony which they held. And they cried with a loud voice, saying, 'How long, O Lord, holy and true, until You judge and avenge our blood on those who dwell on the earth?' Then a white robe was given to each of them; and it was said to them that they should rest a little while longer, until both the number of their fellow servants and their brethren, who would be killed as they were, was completed."
(Revelation 6:9-11)

NO MORE HORSEMEN. The 5th seal is all about martyrdom. After the first four seals are broken, Revelation says there will be a severe persecution of believers all over the world.

The rise of the Islamic Caliphate (1st seal) leads to the Great Pacific War (2nd seal) because the Caliphate, Europe, and Russia will all benefit from the United States being embroiled in a devastating war that reduces its power. For decades, it has only been the strength and influence of the U.S. that has prevented dictators and other immoral powerbrokers from doing as they please.

As we've seen, the Great Pacific War (2nd seal) will likely help cause the Great Depression of Europe (3rd seal) because of the destruction of wheat harvests in the war zones of the 2nd seal.

The oppression of the Caliphate (1st seal), the Great Pacific War (2nd seal), and the Great Depression of Europe (3rd seal) will together create an environment that facilitates the Great Plague of Africa (4th seal) because the demand on doctors from the first three will not leave any left to stop the plague.

All four of these seals will then lead to intense persecution and martyrdoms of Christians (5th seal).

In the Middle East, Christians in tune with God's Spirit will be raising the alarm about Erdoğan being the antichrist and the Caliphate being the Beast of Revelation. In response, Erdoğan himself (if he is indeed the antichrist) would likely martyr millions.

In the United States & China, many believers (yes, estimates say there are 200 million Chinese Christians) will prophesy the coming judgment for their respective countries, urging repentance. They will declare the war to be a hopeless cause, lost before it starts. Survivors will view their predictions as treason and seek to punish them or put them to death.

In Europe, Christians will proclaim that the famine and economic ruin is judgment from God for sin and greed. The European people suffering from severe hunger will not take this well. Believers may be targeted for their money to help "pay for the bread." The large Muslim population in Europe will use the chaos as cover for persecution and killing of Christians and Jews.

In Africa, Christians will be warning that the Plague is a judgment from God. While there will almost certainly be much repentance, there will also be a violent, angry reaction from those who won't repent. There are large contingents of radical Muslims in many African countries, including Nigeria, Sudan, Somalia, Kenya, and others.

Don't Lose Your Faith

If we are right and we are alive when these terrible events begin, you will certainly know believers who are killed. It might even be you.

Some of the first thoughts you may have when hearing the news of your friend's death are: *"How could God allow this?"*, *"Doesn't He love His people?"*, or perhaps even *"Maybe God doesn't care, or isn't even really there."*

This is your moment of faith.

In times such as those, you will be challenged to continue to trust Him. This is why God told us about everything, the good and the bad, ahead of time, so we clearly understand it's all part of His plan.

Let's recall some of the things said about us or our friends who are killed during the martyrdoms of the 5th Seal:

"I saw under the altar the souls of those who had been slain."

John saw their souls under God's altar. This means their death is viewed as a sacrifice for God, something highly valued. Something that will not be forgotten or ignored but rewarded.

"Slain for the word of God and for the testimony which they held."

They were killed for teaching God's Word, for testifying about what God has done in their lives, and for proclaiming God's judgment.

"They cried with a loud voice."

Their call to God is not weak or meek, but loud. These are not insignificant to God, but heard by Him.

"How long, O Lord, holy and true, until You judge and avenge our blood on those who dwell on the earth?"

There is no talk here of turning the other cheek or feeling affection toward those who persecuted them. They're boldly asking God to take vengeance. God does not correct them as if this thing is being asked in the wrong spirit. Instead, He affirms their call, then tells them to be patient a little longer.

"Then a white robe was given to each of them."

They are clothed in righteousness for their sacrifice. To give one's life for Christ rather than give in to the world *is* an act of faith.

Just like Isaac being offered on the altar, so is the self-sacrifice of a believer valuable and strong evidence of a very real faith in God's promises for the Life to come. Faith without works is dead. To sacrifice oneself is a work of faith that lives on forever and is declared righteousness.

"They should rest a little while longer."

The time is close. Once the Great Persecution begins, it is not much longer until the final battle and judgment. Be patient and wait just a little longer.

"Until the number of their fellow servants and their brethren, who would be killed as they were, was completed."

Not all the family has yet arrived for the marriage supper of the Lamb.

If God were to execute His judgment before its appointed time, He would deny the opportunity to the remaining believers to earn their reward and white robe of righteousness. God is giving time so these remaining believers can finish their work of testifying the truth to the world.

"Until the number ... who would be killed ... was completed."

This is a strong teaching. There is some specific number of martyrs that God considers to be *complete*. Meaning, God has already pre-determined exactly how many Christians are to be killed for their testimony, by whom and when.

This is not accidental. God is not surprised by the murder of His children. It's part of the plan.

So, when we hear that our best friend, our parent, our spouse, or our child has been killed by the persecutors, let us not waste time questioning, for it is part of God's pre-determined plan and the ultimate outcome for us and our loved ones is wonderful and good as we live in joy forever more with Him.

Instead, let us have the Spirit of Christ and say, "Father forgive them, for they know not what they do" and witness even more.

THE 6th SEAL

THE GREAT EARTHQUAKE

"I looked when He opened the sixth seal, and behold, there was a great earthquake; and the sun became black as sackcloth of hair, and the moon became like blood. And the stars of heaven fell to the earth, as a fig tree drops its late figs when it is shaken by a mighty wind. Then the sky receded as a scroll when it is rolled up, and every mountain and island was moved out of its place. And the kings of the earth, the great men, the rich men, the commanders, the mighty men, every slave and every free man, hid themselves in the caves and in the rocks of the mountains, and said to the mountains and rocks, 'Fall on us and hide us from the face of Him who sits on the throne and from the wrath of the Lamb! For the great day of His wrath has come, and who is able to stand?'"
(Revelation 6:12-17)

WHEN JESUS breaks the sixth seal, an enormous earthquake shakes the entire world. I see both literal and symbolic messages here.

Physically speaking, the sun's light is being blocked ("black as sackcloth of hair"), and the moon glows red like blood. The stars of heaven fall to the earth, meaning there is some kind of lasting meteor shower, and the sky recedes "as a scroll when it is rolled up."

These signs are all the result of this earthquake. And if *"every mountain and island"* is *"moved out of its place,"* then the earthquake is enormous indeed.

Encircling the entire Pacific Ocean is an enormous series of fault lines and volcanoes called the Ring of Fire. It runs up the entire west coast of both Americas, from Chile to California to Alaska, then over to Russia and all the way down the east side of Asia, including Japan, the Philippines, Indonesia, and New Zealand.[164]

If an earthquake the size associated with the 6th Seal were to happen, it would have to involve the Ring of Fire. Curiously, the Ring of Fire seems designed to accomplish something very peculiar. If such a quake were to erupt along the Ring of Fire, it would maximize damage to the nations touching the Pacific, but cause the least damage to Israel.[165]

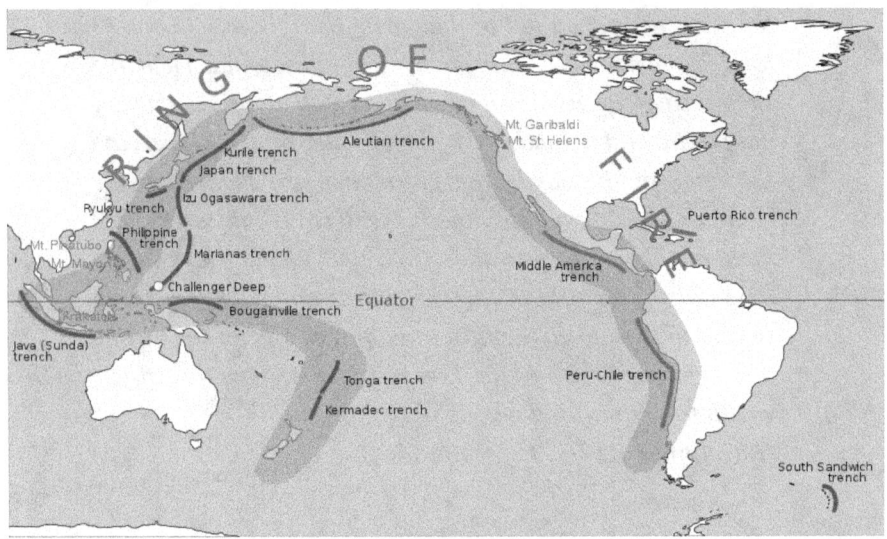

Source: Wikipedia.org

Israel is about the farthest away from it as you can get!

Earthquakes are currently measured on something called the Moment Magnitude Scale. Most people cannot feel an earthquake until it hits the 3.0 range on that scale. This scale is exponential in its numbering, so a 4.0

---

[164] https://en.wikipedia.org/wiki/Ring_of_Fire
[165] https://en.wikipedia.org/wiki/Ring_of_Fire#/media/File:Pacific_Ring_of_Fire.svg

earthquake is 32 times stronger than a 3.0.[166] And a 5.0 is over one thousand times stronger!

For your reference, the earthquake that struck San Francisco in 1989 and collapsed sections of its interstate highways was a 6.9, almost one million times stronger, and the one that just about fully destroyed San Francisco back in 1906 was a 7.9, thirty-two million times larger than an earthquake that can be felt by people. At that strength, the ground actually liquifies in places, causing structures and people to sink into the earth like quicksand.

An earthquake that would move every mountain and island (probably a 10.0 on the Moment Magnitude Scale) would not just be felt around the world, but it would cause major destruction around the world. It would be 1,000 times more powerful than the strongest earthquakes the world has ever felt.

The Sky Recedes Like a Scroll

Imagine slowly losing sight of blue sky as multiple plumes of smoke and ash rise up from different directions simultaneously to eclipse it. This is what the Bible means when it says "the sky receded like a scroll." Billowing clouds of smoke from roll up the blue from both sides until it disappears.

In 1811, there was an earthquake centered in New Madrid, Missouri that measured around 7.9. The quake was so powerful that the ground liquified in places as far away as Georgia and inspired apocalyptic teachings among the Native Americans.

There were no historians to record accounts on the West Coast, but today Californians likely would have felt it as well.

---

[166] https://en.wikipedia.org/wiki/Moment_magnitude_scale

A 9.0 would be felt around the world.[167] A 10.0 would destroy communities around the world and the epicenter would be like a nuclear weapon had gone off.

Such a quake would ignite volcanos around the earth, but especially in the Ring of Fire.

A single volcano can spew enough ash particles into the air to drop temperatures globally by a full degree.[168] If dozens (or even hundreds) of volcanos were suddenly activated, the impact would be impressive.

Volcanic particles would dominate the skyline everywhere. The sky would indeed roll up like a scroll as columns of ash rolled in from every direction.

The sun would be darkened, almost black, like it was covered in a rough cloth. The day would become like night. The particulates in the air would distort the moon's color at night to make it look blood red.

Stars falling from Heaven do remain more of a mystery. However, when this event happens, the exact fulfillment will be clear and obvious.

What's certain is that this will be a very extended meteor shower. It will not be the kind we typically experience where you go outside at night and hope to catch the occasional shooting star.

No, this will be a significant meteor shower that creates fear. It will likely last for at least 24 hours so that every land around the world experiences it. These may even be larger meteors that don't fully burn up and impact the earth strongly enough to kill and destroy.

It's *possible* the entire earthquake is actually created by one huge meteor that strikes on or near the Ring of Fire, launching the massive quake and igniting volcanos. If so, the meteor showers would be the aftermath as the earth passes through the tail pieces of the fallen object.

Contradicting this theory is the fact that in later chapters, Revelation does separately mention large meteor-like objects hitting the earth, yet such things are not mentioned here.

---

[167] http://www.geo.mtu.edu/UPSeis/magnitude.html
[168] https://daily.jstor.org/can-single-volcano-cool-earth/

All of the above is educated guessing. We aren't sure what exactly will happen. What's clear is there will be a very, very large earthquake, overwhelming amounts of ash in the sky, less light, lower temperatures, and some very scary meteor showers.

Spiritual Meaning

The Gospel According to Nature is a book that examines God's symbolism encoded in nature, seeking to understand what spiritual lessons God might have for us to learn by studying His Creation.

From that work, we know that earthquakes represent upheavals and clashes within the Kingdom of God (land), and that volcanic eruptions represent satanic attacks on the Kingdom.

The sun is a symbol for Jesus (the Son), and the moon is God's people (Church/Israel). Light represents truth, warmth represents love, and stars in the sky can represent the individual saints of God, or angels.

Therefore, there is a deeper spiritual meaning behind the actual physical occurrences in this prophecy, as God always intends.

As we established previously, there will already be a Great Falling Away from the Christian faith underway. Even now, throughout the West, Europe, the United States, Canada, Australia, and even Latin America countries are experiencing sharp jumps in the number of people turning their back on God.

When people turn their back on God, some become atheists and leave it at that, but some turn to the occult. These pagan practices can literally crack open the door to hell wider and wider as more and more people engage in the dark arts.

When Jesus begins breaking the seals and catastrophes overtake the earth, more and more people will separate themselves into two clear camps: those who continue to trust God and seek Him, and those who reject Him. Trouble and affliction reveal the true hearts of men, separating the chaff from the wheat. Nobody will be warming the bench anymore. *Everyone* will be playing for one side or the other.

As these two groups solidify, a one-sided, global civil war of sorts will erupt where believers keep turning the other cheek, but anti-Christians keep deepening their hatred.

At the breaking of the 5th Seal, the violence against Christians and Jews explodes.

Such a wide-spread persecution of believers will appear to be a completely *successful* persecution that goes unanswered by God. This will accelerate and amplify the division of people into opposing sides. Many will decide that if God can't protect His people, He must not be real. (Of course, the fact that the Bible predicts this terrible persecution won't be considered.)

It has been said that the blood of the martyrs is the seed of the Church. No doubt this Great Persecution will at the same time inspire others to accept Christ as their Savior when they see believers facing their death fearlessly – even with joy.

On the other hand, those who hate Christians will be emboldened as they persecute, finding themselves less and less hindered from giving in to their baser instincts as believers are removed from society. The spirit of Sodom and Gomorrah will reign, violence and sexual sin will dominate. They will attack anyone who dares oppose them as brutally as their spiritual ancestors tried to do to Lot's visitors in Sodom thousands of years ago.

These radical spiritual clashes within God's Kingdom, which will occur at levels never before seen in history, are symbolized at the breaking of the 6th Seal by the Great Earthquake. Similarly, the increased activity of satan against the Church will be symbolized by volcanic eruptions.

When martyrdoms go unchecked, when justice is absent, and God seems absent, doubt enters. People will severely doubt His presence, His love, His justice, His willingness to act. So, the Sun will be darkened, symbolizing it is harder to see the truth of Jesus (the Son).

None of those truths will have changed, but it will be difficult to "see" them because of the attacks of the enemy (volcanic ash). When we cannot see it, we must have faith the sun is still there.

The warmth of the sun will also be diminished. Global volcanic eruptions will cause temperatures across the world to plummet. In the same way that the Truth of Christ (light) will be blocked by hellish attacks of the enemy (volcanic ash), so will God's Love (warmth of the sun) be less tangible to us. The love of many will grow cold.

The mention of sackcloth is interesting too. Sackcloth is coarse and hairy and quite porous, so the image is a sun that is hazily darkened by smoke and ash but not absolutely blocked like an eclipse.

Sackcloth was traditionally worn by Jewish people in mourning, especially when mourning over sin or tragedy. *So, the sun clothed in sackcloth symbolizes that Jesus (represented by the sun) is heart-broken, mourning over the tragedy that is striking the world and His people.*

The moon turning to blood is a picture of God's people being martyred, covered in blood, especially their leaders who are represented by the face of the moon.

> *"And the stars of heaven fell to the earth, as a fig tree drops its late figs when it is shaken by a mighty wind."* (Revelation 6:13)

There is a different place in Revelation 12 that also references falling stars, but that mention includes a fiery dragon (the devil) casting 1/3 of the stars of Heaven to the earth with his tail. The surrounding verses make it clear those stars represent fallen angels being cast out of Heaven to the earth, along with the enemy.

However, because of the context of Revelation 6:13, these stars seem to be a reference to literal meteors hitting the earth. Yet, because the fig tree is always a symbol for God's people, Israel, *these* stars are symbolically linked to the martyrdom of believers, not the enemy.

NOTE: The global church is typically represented by an olive tree, not a fig tree, so this verse could be saying that the martyrdoms in that moment will be heavy among Israeli Christians (Messianic Jews). However, this remains unclear.

Special Note on the Earthquake

In 1973, a respected and well-known pastor, David Wilkerson, said that he'd had a vision from God and had seen the United States destroyed by a huge earthquake. He has since passed away, but he was not known to be one given to fantastic claims or hyperbole.

In this vision, however, he gave very specific warnings of coming events – catastrophic events – that would be affecting the world in the near future. When recounting what he'd seen, he maintained that he was sure God had shown him this vision and his body language, behavior, and emotions showed he was truly alarmed.

Since that time, some of the specific things he said would happen have indeed happened. We are not saying that we are sure Wilkerson's prophecy is to be considered absolutely true. However, it does give pause.

Note that besides a devastating war, the earthquake described in Revelation 6 is another possible explanation for the destruction of the United States described in Isaiah 18.

At this time, though, we believe the best explanation for Isaiah 18 is one of war, given the many other reasons we've already stated, especially the red horseman going to the ends of the earth.

The Kings of the Earth

They hide in their holes.

> *"And the kings of the earth, the great men, the rich men, the commanders, the mighty men, every slave and every free man, hid themselves in the caves and in the rocks of the mountains, and said to the mountains and rocks, 'Fall*

> *on us and hide us from the face of Him who sits on the throne and from the wrath of the Lamb! For the great day of His wrath has come, and who is able to stand?'"*
> *(Revelation 6:15-17)*

Sometimes phrases in Scripture seem repetitive. We read "the kings of the earth, and the great men, and the mighty men, and the commanders, and the rich men," and we think aren't all those kind of the same thing?

But the Bible never wastes space. When God takes the space to use multiple descriptors like that, there is a reason, even if they seem to be just repeating themselves.

Below is a clarification of what is intended:

- Kings of the Earth (*basileus*) – Sovereign, King, Supreme Leader
- Great Men (*megistanes*) – Noblemen, Politicians
- Rich Men (*plousios*) – Rich Men, Business Executives
- Commanders (*chiliarchos*) – Military Generals
- Mighty Men (*ischyros*) – Physically Strong Men, Special Forces Soldiers
- Slave (*doulos*) – Servants, Employees
- Every Free Man (*eutheros*) – Unbound Man, Small Business Owners, Middle Class

When it comes down to it, most people in the world work in government, the military, or business. So, all of these titles are meant to encompass everyone.

Kings, nobles, wealthy, middle class, poor, generals and soldiers, business executives and employees. Basically, *everyone* is going to try to hide in underground bunkers to hide from the Wrath of the Lamb.

It has been a long practice of governments around the world to build and maintain underground bunkers for emergency protection of their leaders and military.

The United States, Russia, China, the UK, Israel, and others have all constructed massive bunkers for this purpose.[169] Switzerland constructed so many they can now house their *entire population plus some*.[170]

And the practice of building underground bunkers is now going beyond governments. Today, wealthy people around the world are building private hide-out holes like never before. Even everyday citizens (preppers) are getting into the act.[171] [172]

Revelation 6:15-17 begs one question though: How do all these people have time to get to a bunker for safety when the quake hits? Earthquakes hit suddenly and don't necessarily last that long.

One possible answer is that large earthquakes are always accompanied first by precursory quakes and then a ton of aftershocks. A 10.0 earthquake would be so large, it could have dozens of community-destroying 8.0 – 9.0 aftershocks. Such *aftershocks,* by themselves, would be larger than any quake recorded so far in history. The destruction would go on for days and even weeks, so those who aren't killed right away would have time to seek shelter during the aftershocks.

So, the good news for our prepper countrymen building bunkers all over the place is that it looks like they're going to get to use them! The bad news is underground bunkers seem like the worst place to be in an earthquake. I'd rather be in an open field far away from any structures or trees, or in a boat far from shore (just in case the ground liquifies).

Back to the passage, what is even more curious is the people universally cry out, *"Fall on us [mountains] and hide us from the face of Him who sits on the throne and from the wrath of the Lamb! For the great day of His wrath has come, and who is able to stand?"*

---

[169] http://wonderfulengineering.com/10-secret-underground-bunkers-around-the-world-that-will-save-your-life-during-a-nuclear-war/
[170] https://www.swissinfo.ch/eng/prepared-for-anything_bunkers-for-all/995134
[171] https://www.cbsnews.com/pictures/amazing-doomsday-bunkers-of-the-super-rich/
[172] https://www.ussaferoom.com/products/underground-bunker/?gclid=EAIaIQobChMIrc_W4f_Q2wIVCY9pCh3WDwOtEAMYAiAAEgIiiPD_BwE

It's incredible! All the people of the world, at least in this moment, *recognize what is happening.* They see and understand that they are experiencing the wrath of the God of the Bible.

Yet, they don't repent. They don't call out to God Himself to have mercy. They don't cry out to Him for salvation. Instead, they foolishly ask the mountains to crush them to save them from God's wrath.

They are so entrenched in their rebellion that they would rather die than give in to God. And they are so foolish and blind that they think death will somehow save them from Him when it will simply move them directly into their moment of judgment before His throne.

THE 7th SEAL

SILENCE IN HEAVEN

"When the Lamb broke the seventh seal, there was silence in heaven for what seemed like half an hour."

(Revelation 8:1, CJB)

WHEN JESUS breaks the 7th seal, there is silence in Heaven for "about half an hour." This does not mean the judgments of Revelation are stopping. On the contrary, there is much more to come. In the following chapters, we see that following this silence, seven angels begin blowing seven trumpets. A new judgment arrives with each blast.

But why is there silence in Heaven? For what seemed like half an hour?

Honestly, it's unclear. Still, it's a very curious phrase. Clearly, God included it for a reason.

Yet, God's time is not our time, so how are we to interpret it?

Let's notice that while the other seals receive only a few verses of space, during the time between Jesus breaking the sixth and the seventh seals, an *entire chapter* of Revelation plays out: Chapter 7.

In that chapter, God commands the destruction of the earth to be withheld for a time while 144,000 people are "sealed" from the tribes of Israel. What exactly the seal means or represents is not clear. Is it a visible, religious tattoo of sorts that others can see? Is it just symbolic of simple salvations in Jesus? Is it an invisible mark that only angels can see? Or is it an anointing by God for a special mission to testify to the nations?

The latter possibility seems the most likely as Revelation 7:9, 13-14 says:

> *"After this I looked, and there before me was a great multitude that no one could count, from every nation, tribe, people and language, standing before the throne and before the Lamb... Then one of the elders asked me, "These in white robes—who are they, and where did they come from?*
>
> *"I answered, 'Sir, you know.'*
>
> *"And he said, 'These are they who have come out of the great tribulation; they have washed their robes and made them white in the blood of the Lamb.'"*

Therefore, since there is a great and sudden influx of martyrs from the Tribulation from *all* nations, and not just the tribes of Israel, and their numbers are so great they can't be counted, but those sealed from the tribes of Israel were clearly counted, it seems clear that the impact of the 144,000 witnesses from Israel being sealed produces countless new believers from all tribes, peoples and nations.

The silence in Heaven also seems related to this sealing of the 144,000. In Chapter 7, the angels holding back the destructive "winds" are told to wait.

Silence in Heaven means that God is not speaking. That angels are not worshipping as we saw earlier in Revelation. All worship in Heaven pauses, creating a dramatic quiet.

Even conversation between John and the elder or any other angels stops during this time. It feels like an intentional moment of silence respecting the unprecedented number of Christians sacrificing their lives right then for the glory of Christ.

And it's a time when God is briefly pausing the judgments to give one more chance for all those who would come to salvation to repent.

Perhaps once the number of martyrs is complete, the judgments resume and the trumpets begin to sound.

One more note: Elsewhere in Scripture a prophetic day is equated with a year of earth time, i.e. a "week" is 7 years. If we keep with that same ratio, then "half an hour" would correspond to 1 week. This could mean that there is a 1 week pause between the end of the Great Earthquake and its aftershocks and the beginning of the Trumpet judgments.

JESUS AND MATTHEW 24

> *"As Jesus was sitting on the Mount of Olives, the disciples came to him privately. 'Tell us,' they said, 'when will this happen, and what will be the sign of your coming and of the end of the age?'"*
> *(Matthew 24:3)*

WE'VE BEEN VERY focused on the Book of Revelation, but there are other passages that discuss end-times events at length as well. The Books of Isaiah, Jeremiah, Ezekiel, Daniel, Zechariah and others dedicate much space to prophecy of the last days. However, the best passage that could be taken as the clearest, most chronological passage explaining how things will unfold is Matthew 24. There, Jesus Himself tells the disciples what to expect.

So, let's take a look at that chapter, listen to Jesus, and see how it lines up with our chronological view of Revelation.

He begins with:

> *"Jesus answered: 'Watch out that no one deceives you. For many will come in my name, claiming, 'I am the Messiah,' and will deceive many. You will hear of wars and rumors of wars, but see to it that you are not alarmed. Such things must happen, but the end is still to come. Nation will rise against nation, and kingdom against kingdom. There will be famines and earthquakes in various places. All these are the beginning of birth pains.'"*
> *(Matthew 24:4-8)*

Notice the order of the things he says will happen:

1.) False Teachers (Sign of the End Times)

2.) Wars and Rumors of Wars (Signs of the End Times)
3.) Nation against nation (War – 1st & 2nd Seals)
4.) Famines (3rd Seal)
5.) Earthquakes (6th Seal)

We don't see the 4th Seal (Plague) here, but in Luke 21:10, another reporting of Jesus' discourse on the end times, Jesus said "earthquakes, famines and pestilences in various places," so he is referencing all of the seals in Luke at the beginning of his discourse, just as Revelation begins with the seals.

The other missing seal is the 5th one which is the Great Persecution of Believers. But Jesus talks about this next in Matthew 24:9-13:

> *"Then you will be handed over to be persecuted and put to death, and you will be hated by all nations because of me. At that time many will turn away from the faith and will betray and hate each other, and many false prophets will appear and deceive many people. Because of the increase of wickedness, the love of most will grow cold, but the one who stands firm to the end will be saved."*

So, slightly out of order from Revelation, but also not really. We just saw that the Book of Revelation speaks of martyrdoms beginning with the breaking of the 5th Seal, but then in Chapter 7 *right after the earthquake* we see a veritable pandemic of persecution killings with uncountable millions from every tribe and nation reaching Heaven after being martyred.

Therefore, the order is actually the same. Most of the persecution killings come after the earthquake, but rather than confuse the disciples by saying the martyrdoms begin before the earthquake, but really take off after the earthquake, He just speaks of the greater persecution after the earthquake for simplicity sake.

Next, Jesus says:

> *"And this gospel of the kingdom will be preached in the whole world as a testimony to all nations, and then the end will come." (Matthew 24: 14)*

Once again, in Revelation, *after* the seals have been broken, the 144,000 witnesses go out into the world and begin to testify to the nations.

> *"So when you see standing in the holy place 'the abomination that causes desolation,' spoken of through the prophet Daniel—let the reader understand..."*
> *(Matthew 24:15)*

Now, Jesus is speaking of the antichrist standing in the Temple declaring himself to be God. He's also referring to the interactive "image" that the antichrist will place there. We know the antichrist kills the Two Witnesses in Jerusalem in Revelation 11.

If the antichrist successfully kills the Two Witnesses in Jerusalem and is able to prevent anyone from burying their bodies, then he must be controlling Jerusalem completely by that time, which means he also controls the Temple. So, the entrance into God's Temple occurs in Chapter 11.

> *"...then let those who are in Judea flee to the mountains. Let no one on the housetop go down to take anything out of the house. Let no one in the field go back to get their cloak. How dreadful it will be in those days for pregnant women and nursing mothers! Pray that your flight will not take place in winter or on the Sabbath."*
> *(Matthew 24:16-20)*

Revelation 12 describes the severe persecution of the Israeli people that begins right after the antichrist takes Jerusalem. This persecution is directly inspired by the devil and led by his son the antichrist, but Revelation says they flee into the wilderness (desert) and are protected for three and a half years.

We continue to see that the order of events in Jesus' discourse mirrors the order of events in Revelation.

> *"For then there will be great distress, unequaled from the beginning of the world until now—and never to be equaled again.*

> *"If those days had not been cut short, no one would survive, but for the sake of the elect those days will be shortened. At that time if anyone says to you, 'Look, here is the Messiah!' or, 'There he is!' do not believe it. For false messiahs and false prophets will appear and perform great signs and wonders to deceive, if possible, even the elect. See, I have told you ahead of time.*
>
> *"So if anyone tells you, 'There he is, out in the wilderness,' do not go out; or, 'Here he is, in the inner rooms,' do not believe it. For as lightning that comes from the east is visible even in the west, so will be the coming of the Son of Man. Wherever there is a carcass, there the vultures will gather."*
> (Matthew 24:21-28)

Revelation 13 is where we see the antichrist rising toward global power, where the persecution gets so severe that people cannot buy or sell without taking the mark of the beast. This chapter is also where we are introduced to the false prophet who can call down fire from heaven and do other miracles in an attempt to claim to be Jesus Himself returned.

The persecution is so great at this time, Jesus says *"If those days had not been cut short, no one would survive, but for the sake of the elect those days will be shortened"* and *"For then there will be great distress, unequaled from the beginning of the world until now—and never to be equaled again."*

And the false prophet will be so convincing that Jesus says, *"If it were possible, even the Elect would be deceived."* A man claiming to be Jesus, calling down fire from Heaven and performing other miracles with all of the world agreeing that he is Jesus returned? Truly, only those whose eyes are opened by the Holy Spirit will remain free from the deception.

In summary, let's look at the order of events according to the traditionally understood prophetic timeline in comparison with the order of events in Jesus' discourse in Matthew 24 and a chronological reading of the Book of Revelation:

REVELATION UNFOLDING

Traditional Prophetic Timeline	Matthew 24 (Chronologically)	Book of Revelation (Chronologically)
War of Gog & Magog		Arrival of the antichrist
The Rapture	Great Pacific War	Great Pacific War
Arrival of the antichrist	Famine	Famine
Great Pacific War	Plague	Plague
Famine	Great Earthquake	Martyrdoms
Plague	Martyrdoms	Great Earthquake
Martyrdoms	144,000 Witnesses	144,000 Witnesses
Great Earthquake	Antichrist Enters the Temple	Antichrist Enters the Temple
Global Domination of antichrist	Israel Flees	Israel Flees
144,000 Witnesses	Global Domination of antichrist	Global Domination of antichrist
Antichrist Enters the Temple	The Rapture	The Rapture
Israel Flees	Battle of Armageddon	Battle of Armageddon
Battle of Armageddon	Second Coming of Jesus	Second Coming of Jesus
Second Coming of Jesus	1,000 Year of Christ	1,000 Year of Christ
1,000 Year of Christ		War of Gog & Magog
New Heaven & Earth		New Heaven & Earth

If we choose to read Revelation chronologically instead of forcing things into an unnatural timeline, then the two most complete passages in Scripture suddenly agree with each other in the order of events. Most importantly for Christians today, the Rapture happens *after* most of the destructive judgments of the Tribulation.

That means we need to prepare ourselves spiritually.

Conclusion

AFTER READING **this book, you'll likely be filled with a new zeal** to watch for the signs of the end, and even to warn others. And the number one response you will receive from friends and family when trying to talk to them about these things is ... *silence*.

Silence because they don't want to think about these things. It's too depressing. They don't realize that you're actually talking about the end of the bad things of the world and the coming of great things.

People just want to think about what they plan to buy next, their next vacation, and what there is to watch on Netflix. People actually like things the way they are ... as long as the really bad things don't happen to them.

Some will be silent because they think you're ignorant, or just wrong, but they don't want to say it to your face. They don't believe God is ever going to intervene in human affairs. If He's real, they certainly don't think He cares or is that involved in our lives.

If they did believe those things, they would seek Him more.

Others may be bold enough to argue with you or even mock you to your face. When this happens, rejoice for you are seeing honesty. Simply stand your ground and defend what you know to be true, the character and nature of God.

You are looking for those hearts attuned to God who are looking for Him, ready to hear and listen.

I have been very careful in this book not to say that any interpretations herein are absolutely, positively *the* only possible way it's all going to go down. What I am absolutely sure about is that the events described in biblical prophecy *are* going to go down at some point, and in the way that

God has always intended them to. We also believe that it's probably going to happen very soon.

All we have done in this work is to examine the Book of Revelation and other prophetic passages, interpreting them with the best effort possible in parallel with current global events to see if we see anything lining up.

First, we talked about the wrong expectations of many in the United States. American Christians typically believe the antichrist will be a charismatic man of peace who rules Europe and then the world, but that we don't have to worry about him because we'll be raptured before he comes.

We've shown that the truth is the antichrist will be a violent conqueror from Turkey, he will be a Muslim, and the rapture will not happen until way after the antichrist begins his reign of terror. Therefore, we absolutely do need to be on the lookout for him.

We made a list of all the different signs from Scripture of the last days and what we should be looking for. Then, one by one, we showed that all of the Signs of the End Times are in fact true today, and most were not true one hundred years ago.

We examined the Islamic State and how it was a perfect personification of the antichrist spirit and the beast.

Then, we revealed that the true leader of the Islamic State is President Erdoğan of Turkey, and that he deceptively sent the Islamic State in to destabilize Syria and Iraq so that he can likely conquer them in the future. He is currently continuing to increase his military presence in those countries.

We elaborated on all the different prophecies regarding the antichrist in the Bible, as well as the *mahdi* in Muslim prophecy. Erdoğan has not only been declared the mahdi by some Muslim scholars, but he has so far also fulfilled many of the conditions for the biblical antichrist, including his name adding up to 666 in Greek.

To date, no other known person has met all of these conditions in this way.

Lastly, we dug into the Revelation of Jesus Christ and the breaking of the seven seals. We examined those verses closely, along with the 83rd Psalm and the Book of Zechariah, to try and understand better what kinds of disasters would probably be hitting which parts of the world and why.

God gave us prophecy for a reason.

Many Christians act like that reason is either to confuse us or to inspire pointless arguments about things that ultimately don't matter.

But God never does anything that doesn't matter. He specifically spent a lot of time on prophecy in the Bible. He did so to warn us, but He also did it so we would seek Him through seeking answers.

I believe we have found and revealed many good answers for you in this book. May your response not be to rest in this knowledge, but to increase your seeking and love of Him.

May you share your understanding and the love of Christ with everyone you encounter. And may you live it out even better.

Stay tuned for Book 2 as we delve into the Seven Trumpets and the Two Witnesses and the Whore of Babylon.

ABOUT THE AUTHOR

Zack Mason loves the art of the word and the thrill of discovery.

He has been studying Biblical prophecy and world events for over thirty years. This book is the culmination of that effort.

For over twenty years, he has served in leadership in a variety of Christian ministries and is currently the Executive Director of SOF Ministries, an international missions agency involved in work in Central America, Bangladesh, Pakistan, as well as the Executive Director of Path2Hope, an evangelical non-profit that mobilizes the Church within the United States to reach Hurting People with the Gospel of Jesus Christ.

He has a passion for history, languages, travel, and, of course, books.

He currently resides with his family outside Atlanta, GA and plans to continue writing for as long as he is allowed to do so.

www.ingramcontent.com/pod-product-compliance
Lightning Source LLC
LaVergne TN
LVHW051516070426
835507LV00023B/3145